★ ★

You Can Trust

The Communists

(... to do exactly as they say!)

by

Dr. Fred Schwarz

Prentice-Hall, Inc., Englewood Cliffs, N. J.

To Lillian
My wife and unswerving friend

First printing .... August, 1960
Second printing .... October, 1960
Third printing ...... November, 1960
Fourth printing ..... December, 1960
Fifth printing .... February, 1961
Sixth printing .... March, 1961
Seventh printing .... May, 1961
Eighth printing .... May, 1961
Ninth printing .... August, 1961

© Prentice-Hall, Inc.

Library of Congress Catalog Card Number 60-11732

Printed in the United States of America

97677—T

21135

Contents

I

TRUST THE COMMUNISTS?

THE THESIS OF this book is very simple. It is
that Communists are Communists. I intend
to show that they are exactly what they say they are; they believe what they say they believe; their objective is the objective
they have repeatedly proclaimed to all the world; their organization is the organization they have described in minute detail;
and their moral code is the one they have announced without
shame. Once we accept the fact that Communists are Communists, and understand the laws of their thought and conduct,
all the mystery disappears, and we are confronted with a movement which is frightening in its superb organization, strategic
mobility and universal program, but which is perfectly under-
standable and almost mathematically predictable.

In the battle against Communism, there is no substitute for
accurate, specific knowledge. Ignorance is evil and paralytic.
The best intentions allied with the most sincere motives are inef-
fective and futile if they are divorced from adequate knowledge.
Consider a mother who has a small daughter to whom she is devoted. For this daughter she is determined to do all that a
mother may do. She feeds her a well-balanced diet to build a
healthy body; she provides the finest education to develop her
mind; she cares for her spiritual well-being, and gives her a
lovely home. In the environment of this young girl, there are
men who specialize in gaining the confidence of little girls by

giving them candy and enticing them into automobiles to molest them. If the mother neglects to give her child the specific information to meet such a situation, she will fail in her duty, and all her loving care will count for nothing when the crisis comes. There is no substitute for specific knowledge.

It is the purpose of this book to give that knowledge. Some of it is a little technical. Some of it may seem a long way from the everyday needs and activities of life. Nonetheless, the information contained in it is essential to survival.

The statement is frequently heard: "You cannot trust the Communists!" This is incorrect; you can trust the Communists. They are extremely trustworthy. You can trust a cancer cell to obey the laws of its lawless growth. You can trust an armed bank robber to take the money and try to escape. Similarly, you can trust the Communists to act in accordance with the laws of their being.

When people operate according to clearly defined principles, they are both trustworthy and predictable. While we continue to believe that the Communists think, feel and believe as we do, the Communist movement is, as Winston Churchill described it, "a riddle wrapped in an enigma." The movements of the heavenly bodies appeared mysterious and unpredictable till Copernicus discovered the governing laws. When we understand the philosophy of Communism, the unifying purpose concealed in their frequently chaotic and contradictory conduct is revealed.

MARXISM-LENINISM

Nikita Khrushchev said: "Anyone who thinks we have forsaken Marxism-Leninism deceives himself. That won't happen till shrimps learn to whistle." We can trust the Communists to practice Marxism-Leninism.

What is Marxism-Leninism? Stripped to its barest essentials, Marxism is the doctrine of the universality of class warfare, and Leninism is the doctrine of the historic role of the Communist

Party to consummate the universal class war in world Communist victory. The basic doctrine of Marxism-Leninism is that a state of war exists and that the Communist Party has been created to win this war. The war was originally discovered, not declared, by Karl Marx. It is between two classes of society which he called the proletariat and the bourgeoisie. The bourgeoisie is the class of property ownership, the class that owns the means of production. The proletariat he defined as the class of wage labor. Between these two classes, Marx claimed to discover a state of war. The bourgeoisie desires profit; the proletariat desires high wages. If wages go up, profits come down. If profits go up, wages come down. Thus there is a fundamental conflict between these two classes. This conflict Marx called the class war.

Marx taught that the bourgeoisie is the established class in Capitalist society. It has created the State as an instrument to oppress and exploit the proletariat. In reaction the proletariat creates the Communist Party to wage war against the State. Thus the class war manifests itself as war between the Communist Party and the State. With the progress of history, the Communist Party has come to power in Russia, China, and Eastern Europe. The bourgeoisie remains in power in America and her associated allies. Thus the class war has transferred itself from the national to the international plane. The fundamental doctrine of Marxism, therefore, is that Russia and America are at war; that China and America are at war—not that they could be at war; not that they might be at war; not that they will be at war; but that they are at war. This war is historically declared; it is universal; it encompasses every aspect of society; in it there can be no vestige of truce. The Communists did not choose it; they simply recognized it. Their duty is to prosecute the war to total and complete victory.

The weapons of this warfare are not merely the classical weapons of guns, tanks, bombs, and aircraft. The weapons are universal. Education is a weapon; language is a weapon; trade is a weapon; diplomacy is a weapon; religion is a weapon; cultural interchange is a weapon. The Communists view every act and judge every situation as part of the class war. When the Bolshoi Ballet performs in the United States, that is an action in the class war; when a group of American clergymen visits Russia, that is an action in the class war; when the Soviet participates in negotiations for "peace," they fight a battle in the class war. Their participation in the United Nations is part of this warfare. The basic Communist doctrine is: "We are at war!" This is the frame of reference within which every action and thought must be assessed and judged.

It does not take two to make a fight. An idea in the mind of one is enough. Let me illustrate. During the war against Japan, I was a doctor in the Brisbane General Hospital. Brisbane, capital city of the state of Queensland in north-eastern Australia, was the headquarters of General MacArthur and the American troops for the advance to the Phillipines and Japan. Into the hospital, there came one day a man who told me that he had put his finger down his throat to make himself vomit because the Americans were going to poison him. I looked at him in some astonishment.

"How do you know they are going to poison you?" I asked.

"I saw them watching me as I was having my dinner."

"Why are they going to poison you?"

"I don't know."

I sought for an explanation of his attitude. "Has your wife been running around with the Americans?"

That was the only time he showed any emotion. He became quite indignant and said, "Oh, no, nothing like that!"

"They are not going to poison you."

"Yes they are."

"I know they're not."

"I know they are."

He was not angry. He was not yelling, shouting, or screaming. He did not have piercing, staring, penetrating eyes. He had none of the external characteristics of insanity. He looked perfectly normal. Nonetheless, I diagnosed him as a mental case and sent him down to the mental ward. However, he was not a bad case. His wife came in and took him home.

Some days later, an American officer went into a public rest room in Queen Street, Brisbane, and was shot dead with a sawed-off shot gun. His assailant ran away. The police, assuming that the criminal was a man like unto themselves, thinking as they thought, and moved by their motives, investigated without success. They considered the normal motives for murder—robbery, jealousy, revenge, alcoholic fury—but they could not find one clue.

A week later in a suburb of Brisbane, another American officer was killed by the same sawed-off shot gun. This time they caught the assailant. It was the man whom I had treated at the hospital.

He had been working on a baker's delivery van, going from house to house delivering bread to the housewives, handling the money, giving the change, playing with the children. Apparently he was quite normal. But deep down in his conscious and unconscious mind, he believed a lie. He knew the Americans were going to kill him. He wished they were not so determined but he knew they were. A man must protect himself. He took a shot gun, sawed off the barrel, sawed off the stock, and carried it around with him for self-protection. He walked into the rest room. He saw the American officer. He knew his life was in danger. He pulled out the gun, shot the officer dead, and ran for his life. A week later he repeated the same process. He was taken, convicted of criminal insanity, and sentenced to an asylum for the insane.

It did not take two to make a quarrel. An idea in the mind of one was enough. Those American officers had never seen the man in their lives. Towards him they had no attitude except goodwill. But he believed that they were bent on his destruction. Suddenly a gun flashed and a man died. It does not take two to make a quarrel. An idea in the mind of one is enough.

The Communists believe that they are at war with us. This conviction will never be changed in the slightest degree by any action of the Free World. If, tomorrow, the leaders of the Free Nations were to accede to every demand made by the Communist leaders, if they were to neutralize every Strategic Air Command base, if they were to grant the demands on Germany, if they were to neutralize Formosa, if they were to recognize Red China and admit it to the United Nations, if the United States were to withdraw every serviceman and weapon within the borders of continental United States, the Communists would merely believe they had won massive victories in the class war. A step towards our final conquest and destruction would have been taken. We must either recognize this and defend against it, or ignore it and be destroyed. We have no other choice.

PEACE

Since the Communists are at war, they naturally desire peace. Wherever you find a Communist, you find an advocate of peace. "Peace" is one of the golden words of their vocabulary. They have "peace" movements of every kind; they have peace campaigns, peace prizes, peace conferences, peace processions. Every Communist is a devotee of peace.

Most people, watching the military preparations of the Communists, noting the enormous percentage of their budget devoted to military objectives, observing their ruthless, brutal repression of any attempt by their captive nations to secure freedom, classify the Communists as blatant hypocrites. This is far from the truth. The Communists are not hypocrites. They are sincerely and genuinely dedicated to peace. If you gave a mature Communist a lie detector test and asked him if he desired peace with all his heart, he would pass with flying colors. They live for peace; they long for peace; they would willingly die for peace.

What is this peace which they desire? During the war against Japan, most Americans undoubtedly wanted peace. Peace was the thought that comforted mothers whose sons were in danger on distant battlefields; peace was the word which sustained wives, lonely and anxious without their husbands; peace was the goal that motivated servicemen who knew the boredom, the loneliness, and the danger of war. Had they been asked to define peace, they would doubtless have described it as the termination of hostilities in the defeat of the enemy by the allies. Not under any circumstances would victory by Japan have been termed peace. To the American people, peace meant only one thing—American victory. The Communists believe they are at war. They desire "peace" with all their hearts. But to them, peace is that golden consummation when the progressive force of Communism totally overwhelms American imperialism and climaxes in Communist world conquest. By definition, "peace" is Communist world conquest.

Since this is true, any action that advances Communist conquest is a "peaceful" action. When the armies of the Communist Chinese encompass the Tibetans, robbing them of their land and food, stimulating them to frantic, hopeless revolt, and then massacring them, they are consummating peace. When Khrushchev ordered Russian tanks into Budapest to fire into the apartment buildings, reducing them to rubble, entombing man, woman and child, in his heart he had a song of peace.

The Communists use the word "peace" in their own sense with total sincerity. We interpret it in our sense. We are the victims, not of their hypocrisy, but of our own ignorance.

The Communists are not hypocrites. They suffer from paranoic delusions of an intense sincerity. They are so enmeshed in the delusions of Marxism-Leninism that they are beyond the scope of rational argument and conviction. All observed phenomena are interpreted within the framework of their preconceived conclusions. If they were hypocrites, it would be much easier to deal with them. You can make a bargain with a hypocrite; you can scare a hypocrite. When you are dealing with paranoics of highly organized delusional patterns, your sole recourse is to acknowledge and understand these patterns and take appropriate measures to protect yourself against the conduct which results from the delusions.

TRUTH

The Communists invariably tell the "truth," but it is the Marxist-Leninist "truth." Those who believe that the Communists will lie in the interests of Communism are mistaken. In fact, it is not possible for a Communist to lie in the interests of Communism. By definition, if a statement is in the interests of Communism, it is the truth.

Jesting Pilate asked the question: "What is truth?" Christians believe that God is Truth. Truth is a quality of God Himself. An absolute God created an absolute Truth. Truth is. The Communists affirm that this is nonsense. There is no God; there are no absolutes; everything is relative; Truth itself is a relative of the class struggle. Lenin said: "The Communist Party is the mind, the conscience, and the morals of our epoch. Proletarian morality is determined by the exigencies of the class struggle." Truth is a weapon of the class war, and any statement that advances Communist conquest is "true." We can trust the Communists always to say that which will advance Communist conquest. We can trust them always to tell the Marxist-Leninist "truth."

Millions of dollars are being spent on the production of beautiful literature telling this "truth." The truth, according to their literature, is simple: Where Communism comes to power, everyone is happy, prosperous, and free; America, on the other hand, is the vilest, most evil, most degenerate nation the world has ever seen.

An excellent example of the Marxist-Leninist truth is contained in a beautiful, photographic magazine published in English by the Communists in North Korea. Most of the magazine is given over to the portrayal of the radiant happiness and glori-

ous prosperity of North Korea under Communism. Towards
the end, however, they present the picture of America. On a
page entitled "Massacre Committed by American Brutes," there
are six photographs of bodies taken from a mass grave lying
side by side upon the ground. Their relatives weep over them.
Underneath, is the following text:

> Mankind remembers the shocking atrocities the Hitlerites per-
> petrated in the concentration camps in Majdanek and Oswiencim.
> Recently another case of atrocities by the American murderers
> which exceeds in its cruelty the atrocities by the Hitlerites was
> discovered in Korea.
> In a shaft of the Rakyun Mine, Jangyun County, South
> Hwanghai Province, some 800 dead bodies were discovered.
> During their temporary occupation of Jangyun County during
> the Korean War, the American murderers rounded up miners of
> the Rakyun mine and the peasants in the nearby villages and put
> them through severe torture. Then the American devils kicked the
> tortured miners and peasants into the shaft 100 meters deep.
> In the shaft corpses were piled up on top of one another, and
> the torn pieces of the bodies bore bullet holes and scars made by
> the bayonets. Many mothers had their babies tied on their backs.
> The shaft presented a most gruesome scene.
> Honest-minded people can not but hate and condemn the
> American Imperialist murderers whose lust for blood knows no
> end.
> Funeral services for the murdered took place in the Rakyun
> mine in the midst of children's crying for their lost fathers, old
> women wailing over their dead sons. The people's enmity and
> curses upon the American devils rent the air. 'Avenge us of the
> American imperialists!' This was the cry of the 800 murdered.
> But even at the moment in South Korea, the American murder-
> ers are slaughtering our brothers and sisters. This we can not
> tolerate.
> American cannibals get out of Korea immediately.[1]

This is the Marxist-Leninist truth. The objective truth is, of
course, quite different. When the Communists retreated in
North Korea, they took with them all the ablebodied personnel
to serve as laborers. Those who could not stand the rigors of the
northward journey—old men and women, pregnant women,
very young children and babies—they massacred and buried in

---

[1] *Korea*, Vol. 25, 1958, (Pyongyang, Democratic People's Republic of
Korea: Foreign Languages Publishing House).

a mass grave if they belonged to the untrustworthy social classes. The advancing American troops time and again found mass graves filled with the bodies of those murdered by the Communists. The Communists merely disinterred one of their own mass graves, and, with moral indignation, indicted America for it before the conscience of the world. Their moral indignation was real, not simulated. This is almost incomprehensible.

Hitler worked on the principle: Tell a lie, make it big, repeat it often, and the majority of the people will believe you. The Communists have further developed this concept. Any lie that advances Communist conquest is, by definition, not a lie but the Marxist-Leninist truth. The maturity of a Communist can be judged by the extent to which he can divorce himself from the evidence of his senses and totally identify himself with the verdict of the Communist Party. When confronted with a choice between the evidence of his eyes and the verdict of the Communist Party, the mature Communist will believe with such conviction what the Party has said that, were he given a lie detector test, he would pass it with flying colors. He would experience all the emotions associated with truth when he thought of the decision of the Party.

We are astounded when we see evidence of this. An American plane was shot down over Soviet Armenia. The American forces recorded the conversation of the Russian pilots as they shot down the plane. When Mikoyan, visiting America, was confronted with the evidence, he was not confounded in the least. He did not believe it. It was not true. He was a Communist, a Marxist-Leninist. The Communist Party had said that it did not happen, and the verdict of the Party is the Marxist-Leninist truth.

All Communists do not attain this maturity. Many of them would possibly feel a slight element of doubt in such a situation. Final maturity is attained with the ability to identify one's emotions completely with the verdict of the Party.

Communist scientists finally derive their "truth" from the verdict of the Communist Party. Laboratory experimentation is secondary and must be interpreted in accordance with the policy outlined by the Party.

In the late 1940's there arose in Russia a great debate in the realm of Biology. It concerned the question of transmissibility to offspring of characteristics acquired during the life of the parent. Most reputable biologists teach that such characteristics cannot be transmitted.

The Communists attribute this theory to Mendel and Morgan and call it Mendel-Morgan genetics. A Russian biologist, Michurin, developed a theory at variance with this. His theory was advocated by a plant breeder called Lysenko.

The biological section of the Russian Academy of Sciences met to discuss this issue. The Foreign Languages Press of Moscow published a full report of the conference under the title, "Proceedings of the Academy of Science on the Teaching of Academician Lysenko." The verbatim speeches of the leading Russian Scientists were published. Many of these, on the basis of their long laboratory experience, contended that the Michurin-Lysenko school was in error. As scientists, they detailed the evidence on which they based their conclusions.

The issue was resolved very simply. Near the end of the report there is a chapter entitled, "Concluding Remarks of Academician L. D. Lysenko." He reports: "Comrades, the question is asked in a note handed to me: 'Has the Central Committee of the Party adopted any position with regard to your report?' I wish to state that the Central Committee of the Communist Party has read my report and has approved it." (*Prolonged ovation. Great appaluse. All rise.*)

A strange sequence ensues. The leading Russian scientists who had opposed the Lysenko position on the basis of their laboratory experience, had a crisis revelation during the night. The following day, they asked permission to make statements. When permission was granted, they rose and indicated that the error of their way had now been revealed to them. They repented of their former service to imperialist biology and dedicated themselves to true proletarian biology.

The cynic may say: "That is easy to understand. They were scared. They knew what would happen to them if they did not agree with the Party line." However, the question goes deeper than that. They were scientists and they were Communists. They were Communists first and scientists second. As Communists they believed the Communist Party to be "the mind of our epoch," the fountain of all "truth." The verdict of the Party must take precedence over the experience of the senses, even in the scientific experiment.

It may be argued that this situation no longer exists, that things have changed. Russian scientists do not all agree with Lysenko now.

The question at issue is not the rightness or wrongness of the Lysenko theories, but the right of the Communist Party to determine scientific truth by edict. That situation has not changed. Russian scientists may have changed their views, but only because they have been permitted to do so by the Party. "Truth" remains the exclusive province of the Party.

RIGHTEOUSNESS

The Communists demand and develop characters of "righteousness," that is, Marxist-Leninist righteousness. In the book, *How to Be a Good Communist*, Liu Shao-chi, President of Communist China and brilliant theoretical writer says:

> But if sacrifice has to be made for the Party, for class and national liberation, that is, for the emancipation of mankind, for social evolution and for the interests of the greatest majority of mankind embracing countless millions of people, countless Communist Party members will face death with equanimity and make any sacrifice without the slightest hesitation. To the majority of Communist Party members, it will be accepted as a matter of course 'to lay down one's life for a noble cause' or 'to die for righteousness,' if necessary.[2]

---

[2] Liu Shao-chi, *How to Be a Good Communist* (Peking: Foreign Languages Press), pp. 55-6.

What is this righteousness for which they are ready to die? Righteousness is conduct which will advance Communist world conquest. According to this definition, Joseph Stalin was the very personification of Marxist-Leninist righteousness. The many who believe that Khrushchev attacked and condemned Stalin missed the point of his speech entirely. Khrushchev did two things: He described Stalin, and he commended him. His description depicted a man so vile that most folk took it for condemnation. What he said, in effect, was this: Stalin was a murderer; he was not a reluctant murderer, but an enthusiastic murderer. He enjoyed murder. He got a thrill out of the torture of his own friends. When the Jewish doctors were arrested and accused of poisoning Zdanov, Stalin called in the man responsible for examining them and indicated the type of torture to be given each one. He gave three fundamental rules for getting confessions: "Beat, beat, and beat again." He said: "If you don't get a confession by this date, we will shorten you by a head!"

Khrushchev indicated that Stalin was a stark, raving madman. "When you went in to see him in the morning, he would look at you and say, 'What have you been up to? You have a shifty look in your eye today.' You never knew whether you would leave as his friend or under armed guard to be shot." He presents a picture of a murderer of limitless appetite, a picture of megalomaniacal, sadistic madness. But he concludes by saying: "Don't misunderstand me. Stalin was a good man. He was a Marxist-Leninist. He did these things as a Marxist-Leninist." No higher praise could have been given by Khrushchev.

How could he justify both description and designation? Let us project ourselves into the stream of history, and look at Stalin in historic perspective. Stalin assumed power when the Communists were a beleaguered garrison and he brought them to the verge of world conquest. It was Stalin who set up their educational program which today is graduating three times as many engineers and scientists as the American program. It was Stalin who became the patron of scientific research. It was Stalin who established their submarine and missile programs which have caused the shadow of impending death to fall over the life of every person in the Free World. It was Stalin who organized the conquest of China. It was Stalin who deceived American and Free World statesmen. Stalin brought Communism to the very verge of world conquest. A few generations hence, when Communism has conquered the world, and regenerate mankind lives in perfect happiness and complete abundance, the name of Stalin, who did so much to bring this to pass, will be honored and revered. His personal idiosyncracies will be ignored and forgotten. Dead men do not complain. Who worries about last year's fallen leaves? Stalin is the superb exemplar of Marxist-Leninist righteousness.

LOVE

We can trust the Communists to manifest pure, Marxist-Leninist "love." One of the best pictures of Marxist-Leninist "love" was revealed in the boast made by Klementi Voroshilov, now president of Russia, to William C. Bullitt, America's first ambassador to the Soviet Union. At a banquet in Russia in 1934, Voroshilov told Bullitt that in 1919 he persuaded eleven thousand Czarist officers at Kiev to surrender by promising them that, if they surrendered, they, their wives and their families would be permitted to return to their homes. When they surrendered, he executed the eleven thousand officers and all male children, and sent the wives and daughters into the brothels for the use of the Russian army. He mentioned in passing that the treatment they received in the brothels was such that none of them lived for more than three months.[3]

Voroshilov was merely acting in obedience to the dictates of Marxist-Leninist "love." Believing as he believed, he acted in a truthful, righteous, and loving manner. There he stood, one of

---

[3] William C. Bullitt, "A Talk with Voroshilov," printed in *The Great Pretense*, prepared and released by the Committee on Un-American Activities, U.S. House of Representatives, Washington, D.C., May 19, 1956, pp. 18-9.

history's anointed, entrusted with the destiny of world conquest and human regeneration. There stood a group of male and female animals which he could utilize selfishly by keeping his promise to them and making himself feel good in the bourgeois sense, or which he could utilize for the ultimate regeneration and happiness of all mankind by destroying them. His duty lay clearly before him. As a Communist he had no choice. He was nothing; these people were nothing; the will of history was everything. He saw his duty clear. To the executioners went all the males, and to the brothels went all the females. The Red Army was strengthened, world conquest came a day nearer, human regeneration a little closer, and Voroshilov had a conscience as clear as spring water, and a sense of duty nobly done. He was comforted by an acute awareness of the fulfillment of Marxist-Leninist "love."

Communists believe they have a destiny. Their destiny is to create a new world and regenerate mankind. To do this they must conquer the world, shatter the Capitalist system, and, by Communist dictatorship, establish the regenerative environment of Socialism. This new environment will rear the young to perfection.

An inescapable step of their scientific program for the regeneration of mankind is the elimination of the residual diseased social classes following world conquest. A few years ago, the American Communist Party would openly acknowledge that, having conquered this country, they would need to put to death one third of the American people. This is not punishment; it is Social Science. It is not cruelty; it is "love." It is as though the surgeon took the scalpel in a loving fashion to cut away the gangrenous tissue so that the new and perfect might come to maturity.

Communism is applied godless materialism. St. Paul writes:

> Because that, when they knew God, they glorified him not as God, neither were thankful; but became vain in their imaginations, and their foolish heart was darkened. Professing themselves to be wise, they became fools, and changed the glory of

the uncorruptible God into an image made like to corruptible man, and to birds, and fourfooted beasts, and creeping things. Wherefore God also gave them up to uncleanness through the lusts of their own hearts, to dishonour their own bodies between themselves: who changed the truth of God into a lie, and worshipped and served the creature more than the Creator, who is blessed for ever.[4]

Emerging from its lair of godless materialism, dressed in garments of science, Communism seduces the young and utilizes their perverted religious enthusiasm to conquer the world. Building on the doctrines of godless materialism, Communism has completely reversed the meaning of our basic moral terms. When we, in our ignorance of this fact, insist on interpreting their phraseology as if they believed the Christian philosophy from which we have derived our basic concepts, we aid and abet them in their program for our conquest and destruction. Once it is known what the Communists believe, there is no difficulty in understanding, interpreting, and predicting their conduct. On the foundation of knowledge, and on that foundation alone, may an edifice of survival be built.

---

[4] Romans 1:21-25.

II

THE RECRUITING OF A COMMUNIST

IF THERE IS one question asked more frequently than any other, it is this: Why do rich people, educated people, even religious people become Communists? People say, "I can understand the appeal of Communism to the poor, to the ignorant, to the exploited, and to the oppressed. What I cannot understand is its appeal to the wealthy, the educated and the religious. Why do millionaires, college professors, and even ministers of religion become Communists?"

The truth is that Communism as such has little appeal for the poor, the oppressed, or the exploited. The basic appeal of Communism is to the educated, and particularly to the student-intellectual.

A summary survey of leading Communist personalities will soon show that the great majority were recruited as students. While I was in Portland, Oregon, I went to collect my laundry. I mentioned to the laundryman the alarming figures of Communist advance. He had enough intelligence to be alarmed. He said, "We must do something! We must do something!" He thought for a moment and then said, "We must feed them. No man ever became a Communist on a full stomach."

I looked at him and said, "I could mention one or two who did: Karl Marx, Frederick Engels, Vladimir Lenin, Joseph Stalin, Molotov, Bulganin, Kalinin, Mikoyan, Kaganovich, Mao Tse-tung, Chou En-lai, Liu Shao-chi, Chu Teh, Ho Chi minh,

Whittaker Chambers, William Remington, Hal Ware." I ran out of breath, but not out of names. Go to any country in the world, take the outstanding Communist figures, and, if they became Communists in a non-Communist country, you will find almost without exception that they embraced Communism as student-intellectuals.

Consider, for example, the Communist Party of China. The chairman, Mao tse-Tung was converted to Communism at the age of twenty-one while he was student-librarian at the National University in Peking. The Prime Minister, Chou en-Li, son of a wealthy Chinese aristocrat, was studying at a university in Paris, France, when he became a Communist. The commander-in-chief of the Red Army, Chu Teh, son of a wealthy Chinese, was converted to Communism by Chou en-Li while he was studying at a Prussian military academy in Germany. Liu Shao-chi, brilliant theorist and heir apparent to Mao tse-Tung, embraced Communism as a young student. The record is the same wherever you go. The sinister truth is that a majority of the students in the world today are attracted to Communism. Until the appeal of Communism to student-intellectuals is understood, any effort to combat its influence among them is futile.

Following an address at a Baptist school in the South, two students approached me. One was from Mexico, and the other from North Korea. The student from Mexico said, "When I was doing the pre-medical course in Mexico City, 80 per cent of the medical students were Communists. They were organized into cells. Their leaders, utterly godless and materialistic, were trained in Moscow."

Actually, it is doubtful that 80 per cent of the students were really members of the Communist Party. This would be contrary to the Communist concept of a small, elite group which influences, controls, and exploits much larger groups. However, his statement does indicate the powerful influence of Communism among the students of Mexico. The same thing is true in universities in Central and South America, India, Japan, Indonesia, the Near East, Africa, and, in a measure, in Europe and

America. The appeal of Communism to the student-intellectual is extensive and powerful indeed.

It may well be asked why this is so. Some insight into this was given by the second student. He was a refugee from North Korea. America had opened its arms and its heart and had given him refuge. He was surrounded by love and affection; he was well fed and well clothed, an individual protected by the law, significant and important. Despite all this, the ideas the Communists had planted in his mind as a child were still there.

He began immediately to tell me all that was wrong with America, and right with Communism. The trouble with America, he said, was the way the bosses exploited the workers, particularly in the South. American prosperity was a bubble that was going to burst into unemployment, depression, crisis, and civil war. He went on to say that in North Korea, they had New Democracy which was bad, so bad that he had had to flee from it. But New Democracy was going to develop into Socialism such as existed in Russia which was much better. Socialism would finally evolve into Communism which was very good. Under Communism, human nature would be so perfect that there would no longer be the need for any government whatsoever.

The reality had driven him forth in hunger, nakedness and terror, but the vision still lived within his mind.

This student showed rather clearly certain aspects of the appeal of Communism to the student mind. Communism utilizes four things to recruit the young intellectual. These are:

1. Disenchantment with capitalism
2. Materialist philosophy
3. Intellectual pride
4. Unfulfilled religious need.

CAPITALIST DISENCHANTMENT WITH CAPITALISM

The first step in the making of a Communist is disenchantment with the Capitalist system. According to the Marxist analysis

of Capitalism, depression and war are the inevitable consequences of the Capitalist system. Capitalism is also the creator
of vice, crime, and all the evils of society. This has been the
great recruiting doctrine of Communism. Whittaker Chambers
said that every intelligent person of his acquaintance who became a Communist did so in terms of the Marxist analysis of
Capitalism as the creator of depression and war. Once they accepted the Marxist thesis that Capitalism caused recurrent depression and war, it was a short step to the acceptance of the
Leninist program for the destruction of Capitalism.

The Marxist analysis, superficially, is very convincing. Marx
taught that the Capitalist system does two things: it produces
commodities for distribution, and it circulates purchasing
power or money. In other words, Capitalist society is built upon
the production of commodities to be exchanged for money and
the distribution of money to secure those commodities. Capitalist society is healthy, according to Marx, when the amount of
money available to the people is adequate to buy the commodities produced.

Marx contended that, by the very nature of Capitalism, this
balance between goods produced and money available cannot
be maintained for very long. A certain sequence of events is inevitable. The goods produced have a certain money value. That
money is distributed in two ways: the major portion is paid out
in wages to the workers who manufacture the goods—to the
directors, the supervisors, and all the laborers down to the jan-
itor; a smaller portion is retained as profit by those who own the
means of production. During the early stages of the industry,
the money paid to the owners as profit goes into circulation, because new capital goods such as buildings and machinery are
necessary. Since these capital goods are produced and are not
available for purchase by the mass of the people, the wages paid
to the workers producing these capital goods are used to buy
consumer commodities. During the period of capitalization,
there is usually enough money in circulation to buy the consumer goods produced. But eventually the point is reached

where there are enough factories and machinery, and there is no longer need for this expenditure. The profit is then retained and accumulated in bank balances, and the only money circulated is the money paid in wages for producing the goods. Since this is never quite enough to buy the goods produced, production inevitably leads to over-production.

At first this over-production is small and almost unnoticeable, but gradually it becomes more significant. The warehouses of the manufacturers become filled with goods, the inventories of the distributors are complete, and the point is reached where the factory has enough goods on hand to supply the demand for some considerable period. When that point is reached, alternative courses of action present themselves. The manufacturers may say, "Now, the real trouble is that people haven't enough money to purchase these goods. We had better find some way in which people can get more money." On the other hand, they may say, "We have enough goods now. We do not need to make any more for a certain period. We had better cease production until our surplus is used up." The normal process is to follow the latter course and to lay off the workers. When they are laid off, the purchasing power is further reduced, and the situation becomes worse.

According to Marx, this cycle is inevitable. Production leads to over-production which leads to unemployment. This leads to reduced purchasing power, which aggravates the entire situation by accelerating the accumulation of surplus products and leading to further unemployment. The eventual outcome is depression and crisis. Warehouses are filled with goods which the people cannot buy. The economy stagnates and grinds to a standstill.

When this happens, a method must be found whereby purchasing power is once again given to the people that the goods may be bought and that the wheels of the economy may begin to roll once again. Historically, one method has always put money in people's pockets without simultaneously creating consumer goods. That method is war. A war breaks out on some pretext or another. Money is found to finance the war; the wheels of industry begin to turn on war production; money is distributed to the people, and the surplus consumer products are purchased. When the surplus is consumed, normal production begins again, and the cycle goes on, repeating itself again and again. According to Marx, therefore, as long as Capitalism continues, there will be recurrent crises of depression and war.

This seems a powerful and convincing argument. It is the more dangerous because it is, like most Marxian arguments, a half-truth. By taking some of the variables in the situation and concentrating on them, it produces conclusions which appear very sound. These conclusions, however, are not necessarily valid, for there are many important factors which are ignored.

In the first place, Marx's argument is merely diagnostic. Even if it be assumed that his diagnosis is accurate, it does not necessarily follow that the treatment prescribed by the Communists is correct. Other groups who accept the Marxian analysis of Capitalism have completely different prescriptions for treatment. Social Credit devotees, for example, say that the problem is not over-production, but lack of purchasing power. Therefore the amount of surplus production should be assessed periodically, and a national dividend declared corresponding to the surplus. This money, given to the people, can be used to buy up the surplus and production will continue.

In the second place, the argument ignores many most important factors in distribution. Although this is not a textbook of economics, some of these ignored factors should be mentioned. They are:

1. The dynamic nature of money
2. The role of psychology in the economy
3. The relation of advertising to distribution
4. Consumer credit
5. Continually expanding market
6. People's capitalism
7. The role of government and legislation

1. The Dynamic Nature of Money

Money is not static. The same amount of money spent three or four times will distribute three or four times as many goods. There is an intriguing story about a man who wrote a check for a hundred dollars without having any money in the bank. With it he bought a certain article. The man from whom he purchased the article took the check and, without cashing it at the bank, used it to purchase certain goods. These he sold for one hundred and twenty dollars, making a profit of twenty dollars on the deal. The person to whom he gave the check did likewise. This happened ten times, each person making a profit of twenty dollars, before the check finally reached the bank where it was dishonored. The ten people who had handled it got together and decided that to avoid trouble, each of them would contribute ten dollars to cover the check. This was done; the hundred dollars was paid; and each of them was richer by ten dollars. This story simply illustrates that the question of credit and rate of circulation of money must be considered.

2. The Role of Psychology in the Economy

Suppose everyone is persuaded that a depression is coming and decides not to buy another automobile for twelve months. The result would be an immediate depression in the automobile industry with all the consequences that follow. It is quite obvious that the psychological attitude of the people has a tremendous bearing on the economic situation of a country. This is an aspect of economic theory to which Marx gave little attention.

3. The Relation of Advertising to Distribution

The question of the psychological outlook of the consumer naturally leads to the question of advertising and its role in distribution. During the recession in 1958, this factor was understood more completely and a campaign started urging people to buy. The recession did not develop into a depression. The Marxist cycle was broken.

Marx himself cannot be blamed for his failure to consider the role of advertising as the advertising industry was not in existence during his lifetime. It is the followers of Marx who are culpable in this respect.

4. Consumer Credit

An outstanding development of modern Capitalism is consumer credit. Goods are purchased not with money presently owned, but by a promise to pay in the future. This has become such a large factor in the economy that any analysis which does not consider this is obviously fallacious.

5. The Continually Expanding Market

Human aspirations are limitless, and under a free economy these form a continually expanding market. A large percentage of American industry now produces items that did not even exist a few years ago. The vast electronic industry, for example, has been a very recent development. The double-car garage is now as normal to the modern home as the faucet with running water. Soon the motorboat will be the routine companion of the car.

6. People's Capitalism

Possibly the most devastating repudiation of the Marxist doctrine is the development of people's Capitalism within the United States. Marx foresaw the wealth of the community being concentrated in fewer and fewer hands. The class owning this wealth he called the bourgeoisie, and the natural forces within Capitalism would constantly diminish the number of this class.

Contrary to the expectations of Marx, the ownership of American industry is constantly enlarging. There are now nearly as many stock holders in the United States as there are members of organized labor. It is quite conceivable that in a short period, the number of stock holders will exceed union membership. The profits received by the vast majority of these stock holders are utilized for purchasing.

This renders the whole argument of the "class war" ridiculous. Nothing does such damage to the principles of Marxism as the development of worker ownership in American industry. Proletarian stock holders certainly make the concept of universal class war somewhat ludicrous.

7. The Role of Government and Legislation

Finally, the Marxist analysis ignores the role of government and legislation in relation to the economy. The anti-trust laws have restrained the development of monopoly within the American economy. Whatever the individual viewpoint of the role of government in economic affairs, it is a factor which cannot be ignored.

In spite of the foregoing, the Marxist analysis has convinced many people. It would be a simple matter to go before any inexperienced student group and, taking them unprepared, convince practically every one of them that the Marxist argument is sound. This is what the Communists have done. Students throughout the world are being taught as a basic principle that the Capitalist system is evil and the creator of depression and war. Disenchantment with the Capitalist system is the first step in the conversion of a student-intellectual to Communism.

If the situation is considered objectively, it will be seen that there is much to be said in support of Capitalism. The Capitalist system has produced more goods, provided a more equitable distribution, and maintained a higher level of personal freedom than any other system in the world has been able to do.

The Korean student who spoke to me said, "Of course, in America there is far more freedom than anywhere else."

"That's interesting," I replied. "How did the American people get that freedom?"

He looked at me, puzzled.

"Let's think about it for a while," I said. "The freedom in America has a material and a spiritual foundation. The material foundation is the efficient production of goods in quantity and their extensive distribution is so that most people have the material requirements of freedom—sufficient food, shelter, clothing, transportation, and other necessities. The material system within America has produced more food, clothing, and shelter per individual than any other system. Add to this material abundance the spiritual concept of man as the child of God, created, loved, redeemed, infinite in value, and possessed of certain inalienable rights. The result is this freedom you admire."

Then I asked, "What is the material system that has produced these goods in such quantity and distributed them so widely?"

"I don't know," he replied.

"You most certainly do know. You have been telling me for half an hour how bad it is. It is the Capitalist system. Did it never occur to you that maybe the Capitalist system that you abhor so much stands in causal relationship to the freedom you cherish so highly?"

He was lost. This had not been part of the closed circle of argument that he had heard. His arguments were all worked out and complete. These new ideas came in and shattered the symmetry and perfection.

The idea of collective ownership fascinates some people, but its benefits are a mirage. The story is told of a visitor to a Russian factory who asked the workers, "Who owns this factory?"

"We do," they replied.

"Who owns the land on which it is built?"

"We do."

"Who owns the products of the factory when they are made?"
"We do."

Outside in a corner of a large park were three battered jalopies. The visitor asked, "Who owns those cars out there?"

They replied, "We own them, but one of them is used by the factory manager, one is used by the political commissar, and the other is used by the secret police."

The same investigator came to a factory in America, and said to the workers, "Who owns this factory?"

"Henry Ford," they replied.

"Who owns the land on which it is built?"

"Henry Ford."

"Who owns the products of the factory when they are made?"

"Henry Ford."

Outside the factory was a vast park filled with every make and variety of modern American automobile. He said, "Who owns all those cars out there?"

They replied, "Oh, we do."

You may take your choice but, personally, give me the automobile.

The concept that Capitalism is inherently evil and collective ownership inherently good is contradicted finally by one unanswerable fact. Wherever Communism is in power, the people flee by the millions. They leave everything they love, and they flee to loneliness and the unknown to escape the horror of life under Communist rule.

On the other hand, when all the evils of the Capitalist system have been admitted, the fact remains that every year multiplied thousands risk their lives, not trying to get out of America, but trying to get in. They swim the Rio Grande River. Their goal is not to live at America's highest standard, but to live at her lowest. On a comparative basis, the economic system of competitive free enterprise has produced abundance and liberty and is a magnet to the less fortunate.

Many students, however, have a sense of shame concerning Capitalism. They have been convinced by Communist arguments that the Capitalist system is evil, that it has failed, and that it must be replaced. Once convinced of this, a student has taken the first step towards becoming a Communist.

MATERIALIST PHILOSOPHY

The second factor in the creation of a Communist is materialist philosophy. The student-intellectual is taught that there is no God; that matter in motion is the sum total of all being; that each individual is a body in which a stomach secretes gastric juices, a liver secretes bile, and a brain secretes emotion and thought. There is no soul; there is no spirit; there is no heaven to gain, no hell to shun. A new scientific age has been born, and the need for God has been abolished. The modern outlook is materialism.

Speaking at a university, I outlined these basic, Communist materialist beliefs of communism:

(a) Godlessness

(b) The material nature of man

(c) The environmental nature of man's intellectual and so-called spiritual qualities.

A woman jumped to her feet and said, "Why, I hear these things taught in this university every day. The professor of psychology goes to the board and draws a diagram. He says, 'You are only a machine. You are no more and no less. You are a pattern of conditioned behavior. The machinery of your body is very complex. Indeed, your brain is so complex that it gives the impression of freedom, choice, and volition. But actually, you are as automatic as an automobile. You have no soul, you have no spirit, and, in the last analysis, you have no mind.' He laughs at God and he laughs at morality."

That man is not necessarily a Communist. He may even consider himself an anti-Communist. But every student who believes what he teaches will find the Communist program logical and appealing. For Communism carries this teaching to its logical conclusion.

Communism says that every characteristic and attitude of the human personality emerges from the brain. The brain is formed by the accumulation of experiences in the form of conditioned reflexes. These experiences are provided by the environment which is predominantly economic. What we think, what we feel, what we believe, whom we love, and whom we worship merely reflect our economic environment.

Once you accept this, it follows, as night follows day, that if you can control completely the environment, you can generate the mind and character you desire. Thus Communism becomes a program for scientific, materialistic regeneration.

This program for regeneration opens a wonderful vista for the human mind. The Russian Communists already claim to have successfully regenerated many people. One book they have published is entitled *Peoples Regenerated*. They claim they will produce perfect people with perfect bodies, perfect minds, and perfect characters, living together in perfect happiness. This is to be done by means of science.

The first step in the program is to face realistically the scientific needs. The present environment is Capitalistic and evil, creating degenerates, criminals, and sundry vicious characters. While that environment continues, human nature cannot be changed. To try and persuade people to be different while they live in an environment that determines how they act is fatuous nonsense. It is like trying to dry the baby while he is still lying in the bath water. To be successful, you must take him out of the water first. Similarly, if man is to be changed, he must be removed from his Capitalist environment. To do this, the Communists must conquer the world and utterly destroy the Capitalist environment. Capitalism will then be replaced by Socialism which is built not on profit, greed, and self, but on service, cooperation, and others.

In the new environment of Socialism, the babes will receive

new experiences which will condition them to unselfish, voluntary service. The babes will grow to children, the children to adolescents, and the adolescents to adults. How different things will be! Everyone will work because he loves to work. Everyone will give because it is better to give than to receive. The hand of none will be raised in anger against his brother. No longer will there be need for a police force, for there will be nothing for the police to do. There will be no income tax to pay, because people, working willingly, skilfully, and creatively, will produce total abundance, but will partake merely to the extent of their limited needs. All that mars the happiness of man will be gone forever. Vice, crime, famine, pestilence, and war will be merely words from a forgotten past, while abundance, brotherhood, and mutual, co-operative service will bind lives together in the golden day of Communism that has dawned upon the earth.

Frequently after depicting this promise of Communism, I am accused of making it appear too attractive. This is exactly the way it appears to the student. That is why student-intellectuals join the Party. This is just how Communism is presented to them, and on their materialist foundation, it is logical. Liu Shao-chi in his book, *How to Be a Good Communist*, writes:

> What is the most fundamental and common duty of us Communist Party members? As everybody knows, it is to establish Communism, to transform the present world into a Communist world. Is a Communist world good or not? We all know that it is very good. In such a world there will be no exploiters, oppressors, landlords, capitalists, imperialists or fascists. There will be no oppressed and exploited people, no darkness, ignorance, backwardness, etc. In such a society all human beings will become unselfish and intelligent Communists with a high level of culture and technique. The spirit of mutual assistance and mutual love will prevail among mankind. There will be no such irrational things as mutual deception, mutual antagonism, mutual slaughter and war, etc. Such a society will, of course, be the best, the most beautiful and the most advanced society in the history of mankind. Who will say that such a society is not good? Here the question arises: 'Can Communist society be brought about?' Our answer is 'yes.' About this the whole theory of Marxism-Lenin-

ism offers a scientific explanation that leaves no room for doubt. It further explains that as the ultimate result of the class struggle of mankind, such a society will inevitably be brought about.[1]

It is on the foundation of materialism that this scientific program for human regeneration is built.

There are, of course, one or two unpleasant steps on the way to this glorious goal. One of these is the problem of dealing with those who populate the world when the Communists conquer it. These people, formed in the old environment, will think, feel, love, and worship in an established pattern. If they are allowed to raise their young, they will reproduce in them their own qualities, and the Communist aim of generating new characters and perfect human society will be thwarted. Obviously, therefore, they cannot be allowed to remain where they are.

Some of them will be segrated and used to do some useful work until they die. Some of them can be re-educated in reeducational institutions, namely, the labor hospitals. The disease of Capitalist character, according to the Communists, is determined by the false labor relationships of the Capitalist system. In Capitalist society, labor is associated with profit or reward, whereas labor should be its own reward. The unfortunate victims of Capitalist society will be taken in their diseased state, and put into Communist institutions of pure labor. There they will rise in the morning to labor, and will go to bed at night weary and exhausted with never a thought of any reward. The therapeutic of labor will cure them of their grievous Capitalistic disease. The Communists consider themselves humane in the extreme for providing these therapeutic institutions of labor to regenerate diseased Capitalist mankind. It is our bourgeois ignorance that causes us to classify them as slave labor camps.

It is only the young, however, who merit the curative process. The older members of the diseased classes who are established in their ways must obviously be destroyed. This the Communists believe to be their duty. Such people would not be happy

---

[1] Liu Shao-chi, *How to Be a Good Communist* (Peking, China: Foreign Languages Press, 1949), pp. 37-38.

in the new environment. It is kindness to destroy them—a type of social euthanasia. The Communists have no conscience about it because, according to their materialist philosophy, it is but a step towards the glorious goal of the regeneration of all mankind. This step may seem a little unpleasant if bourgeois sentimentally persists, but it is quite necessary to the process of regenerating mankind.

The record of Communism is one of recurrent fratricide and genocide. Their contempt for individual human life has known no bounds. Whether the life to be sacrificed was that of friend or foe appears to have been immaterial. The Communist Party of Russia devoured its own creators. Stalin put to death a majority of the original Bolsheviks. The Communists destroyed not only landlords and Capitalists, but peasants and workers, Kalmucks and Balts with equal ferocity. In spite of knowing this, the allegiance of many educated, apparently cultured American Communists has not been shattered. Many people are amazed that they do not turn from Communisn in loathing and repulsion when confronted with its unutterable barbarism, brutality, and intellectual prostitution.

To the dedicated Communist, however, these are but the temporary necessary sacrifices which the glorious future demands. To wipe out the residual Capitalist debris is not murder but social science. Since any individual man is a mere historic accident, an undergraduate beast, it is stupid to regard him as of infinite value. It is the species and the class that are important. The Capitalist class has been rejected of history and must be destroyed.

Capitalism in America has developed to a greater degree than Capitalism in many other countries. Therefore the number infected by the Capitalist virus is larger than in other lands. A greater program of elimination will thus be needed. It is probable and natural that, should Communism prevail in America, a program of class liquidation will ensue that will dwarf similar programs in other countries.

To those Capitalists who can regard the triumph of Communism with equanimity, I would ask the question: What will be your attitude when you and your family face destruction because of your membership in the historically rejected Capitalist class? As the wide-bore revolver with the soft-nosed bullet is placed at the nape of your neck to shatter your pattern of Capitalistically conditioned reflexes into a bloody oblivion, will you be able to comfort your dying hours with the thought that you are dying in a good cause, in the interests of the scientific regeneration of the animal species *homo sapiens* and the birth of the classless society?

INTELLECTUAL PRIDE

A third factor in the making of a Communist is intellectual pride. The student of eighteen or nineteen years of age is beginning to feel the freedom of his new intellectual environment. He is just beginning to realize how little his parents know. For sixteen or seventeen years the truth of their backwardness and ignorance passed him by, but now the light is dawning. He has come to realize the sordidness of the traditions of his own country and to discover that national heroes, even men like Washington and Lincoln were motivated by personal, selfish greed. Becoming disenchanted with his family and national heritage, he is ripe for conversion to Communism. Convinced of his intellectual brilliance, he sees himself as master of the situation, as one who is entitled, because of his superior intelligence, to be the executive of the great program for the regeneration and perfection of all mankind. Mankind certainly needs changing, and he is just the man to do it.

UNFULFILLED RELIGIOUS NEED

The fourth factor in the making of a Communist is unfulfilled religious need. "Man shall not live by bread alone." Life needs a purpose. Man is born with a heart to worship God, to reach out for something bigger and beyond himself, to seek some noble vision for which to sacrifice, some purpose for which to live and die. When denial of the existence of God deprives him of his natural fulfillment, Communism provides a substitute. It gives him a sense of purpose and destiny, gives meaning to life, and provides a motive for sacrifice.

People are mystified when a man born to great wealth and social position becomes a Communist, spends his fortune for Communist purposes, and even goes to jail in the interests of the Communist cause. To many people, this does not make sense.

Let us try to put ourselves in his position. As a child he has the finest tutors. He is very intelligent. Very early in life he learns that there is no God, that the idea of God is for dull and second rate minds, and that he, in the purity and perfection of his intellect, has no need for God. He accepts the Darwinian hypothesis concerning the origin of man, and the Marxian hypothesis concerning the origin of civilization, culture, morality, ethics, and religion.

As a young man he sits on the mount of learning and watches the progress of the animal species from the jungles via savagery and barbarism to civilization. He watches the productive forces as they operate on the human species dividing it into nations and classes, creating cultures, civilizations, moral codes, educational and political institutions and religious faith. He sits above it all, and beyond it all. He is lost in lonely isolation. Life is devoid of meaning, purpose, and objective. Yet he is a young man with all the idealism and emotional urgency of youth. Where can he find fulfillment? Some seek it in sporting life; some in the life of a playboy. These outlets have little appeal for him.

Suddenly he hears a whisper on the breeze that history in the goodness of its heart is calling unto itself a few of its finest and its best—superior intellects, courageous characters with an insight into its mind and its purpose, and a knowledge of historic law and historic will; that it is uniting them into its finest organization and giving them the destiny of conquering the world and regenerating mankind. It comes as a vision of glory. It sets a song singing in his heart. It puts stars before his eyes. It leads him forward to live and, if necessary, to die in the Communist cause. In it he finds a religious refuge for his godless and unbelieving heart.

Communists are not born; they are made. They are being formed constantly on the campuses of the world. As long as youth is disillusioned, materialistically orientated and spiritually unfulfilled, there will be no dearth of Communist recruits. Herein lies our greatest challenge.

III

THE MOLDING OF A COMMUNIST—
Communist Party: Origin and Organization

THE ACHIEVEMENTS of Communism are unprecedented in the annals of human history. The Communists have repeatedly achieved the impossible. They have made idiots of every expert. Any man who had predicted twenty years ago, the situation that exists in the world today, would have been laughed to scorn. How have they done it? What force has been let loose upon the world?

The achievements of Communism are the achievements of organization. The Communist Party was formed, not on a principle of economic doctrine or philosophy but upon a principle of organization. Communism is the great illustration of the truism that organization will inevitably conquer disorganization and spontaneity.

ORIGIN

Karl Marx and Frederick Engels were the authors of the basic philosophic and economic Communist doctrines. They lived and wrote from about 1840 to 1890. During their lives, many movements were formed to advance Marxist teachings. A Marxist party was finally formed in Russia under the name of the Social Democratic Labor Party. The individual largely responsible for its formation was a man called Plekhanov.

In 1903 a conference of the Russian Social Democratic Labor Party was held in Brussels, Belgium. The police, objecting to this international gang of racketeers and revolutionaries meeting in their fair city, asked them to move, whereupon they went across to London, England, the historic haven of refugees. This congress in 1903 is one of the significant events in world history.

A young man named Vladimir Ilyich Lenin came to the congress with very definite ideas about the type of organization that was necessary to achieve basic Marxist objectives. Lenin desired a party organized on military lines, composed of professional revolutionaries subject to maximum discipline and indoctrination. He desired a party of total obedience and submission that would operate with a single mind and will. At the congress, he introduced a motion to implement his ideas concerning the nature of the Party. He moved that no one be accepted as a member of the Party unless he served in a disciplined capacity in one of the Party organizations. A man could not come and say, "I approve the doctrines, the aims and the methods of your Party. I'd like to join. I'll pay my membership dues. I'll abide by the rules. Sign me up." This was not the way it was to be done. Lenin declared that if a man wished to join the Party, he should first link up with one of its working units. The Party operated through multiple local organizations. Some of these units met in neighborhoods, others met in factories, while still others met in the military forces. Having joined one of these units, the individual could prove himself by working within it in a disciplined, obedient fashion. Only in this way should he come into Party membership.

Lenin's motion was opposed by Martov who approved the idea in principle, but who thought it a little too extreme. He pointed out that there were certain important individuals who would be embarrassed if they had to serve in a humble, disciplined capacity in one of the Party organizations—such people as members of the aristocracy, important businessmen, leading government servants, university professors. Many of these people approved of the Party and were willing to support it, but they would be embarrassed if they had to join a street corner group and engage in its activities. Therefore he suggested a special clause that would allow general membership for special people who could come into membership without joining one of the working units.

Lenin, however, stood firm, insisting that they did not want such people. They needed a party of unity, discipline and obedience, with every member under observation and control. Those unwilling to join on these conditions could become sympathizers and helpers, but they must remain on the outside. The Party wanted no member who was not totally subject to Party discipline.

The vote was taken and Lenin obtained a majority. The Russian word for majority is akin to "bolshevik" and the word for minority is akin to "menshevik." The followers of Lenin became known as the Bolsheviks, and those of his opponent, Martov, were known as the Mensheviks.

It was a seemingly unimportant difference of opinion concerning Party membership, but the cleft that it caused has become the determinant of the destiny of the world. Neither Lenin nor Martov realized its depth and significance. They held unity conferences periodically, but there were quarrels and the cleft widened. In 1917 the division became formal and final. In that year, Lenin returned to Russia from exile in Geneva, Switzerland, after the revolution that had overthrown the Czar, and renamed the Bolshevik segment of the Russian Social Democratic Labor Party the Communist Party of Russia (Bolshevik). From that tiny fragment, the entire present world Communist movement has developed.

There has never been any growth like that of the Communist Party in the history of mankind. Some measure of its growth is revealed by the fact that, in one generation, the Communists have conquered more people than Christians have even told about Christ after nearly two thousand years. Some measure of their progress is indicated by the fact that today there are five children in school learning in detail the godless doctrines of Communism for every one child in school learning anything about Christ. The success of the Communist Party has been due to the ceaseless activity of this Leninist organization.

The first step is the recruitment of an intellectual elite to be the core of the Communist Party. The idea is not to recruit great masses of people. The concept is that of a disciplined and dedicated minority who conquer the masses by reason of their superior knowledge and organization. Some of the influences that lead to the recruitment of the intellectual have already been discussed. It is no light thing to join the Communist Party. The membership price is very heavy. It is yourself. Everything you are and everything you hope to be is given utterly to the Communist Party. Some idea of the concept that the Communists have of their role and destiny is given by the speech of Joseph Stalin on the death of Lenin.

> Comrades, we Communists are people of a special mould. We are made of a special stuff. We are those who form the army of the great proletarian strategist, the army of Comrade Lenin. There is nothing higher than the title of member of the Party whose founder and leader was Comrade Lenin. It is not given to everyone to be a member of such a party. It is not given to everyone to withstand the stresses and storms that accompany membership in such a party. It is the sons of the working class, the sons of want and struggle, the sons of incredible privation and heroic effort who before all should be members of such a party. That is why the Party of the Leninists, the Party of the Communists, is also called the Party of the working class.
>
> Departing from us, Comrade Lenin adjured us to hold high and guard the purity of the great title of member of the Party. We vow to you, Comrade Lenin, that we will fulfil your behest with credit.[1]

In his book, *How to Be a Good Communist*, Liu Shao-chi, President of Communist China, outlines the qualities demanded of a Communist.

---

[1] *Selected Works of V. I. Lenin* (Moscow: Foreign Languages Publishing House, 1952), p. 21.

Whether or not a Communist Party member can absolutely and unconditionally subordinate his personal interests to the Party's interests under all circumstances is the criterion with which to test his loyalty to the Party, to the revolution and to the Communist cause.

To sacrifice one's personal interests and even one's life without the slightest hesitation and even with a feeling of happiness, for the cause of the Party, for class and national liberation and for the emancipation of mankind is the highest manifestation of Communist ethics. This is a Party member's highest manifestation of principle. This is the manifestation of the purity of proletarian ideology of a Party member.[2]

The demand is for absolute and unconditional subordination of personal interests to the Party's interests under all circumstances. The Communist must not only be prepared to die for Communism, but he must feel happy while he is dying. Lenin defined Communists as "dead men on furlough." The Communist dies to self, and gives the Communist Party his life.

ORGANIZATION

The principle of Communist Party organization is known as "democratic centralism." The Party, at the base, is made up of local units, each containing a small number of people. This unit, may be called a cell, a club or any innocuous name. It may be a neighborhood group, a factory group, a school group or a nationality group. Each local group elects a representative to a district council which co-ordinates the actions of the local units. This election of representatives is the democratic aspect of the organization. However, the local unit may not instruct its representative how to vote at the district council. Once elected, he is responsible to the district council, not his local group.

When the district council meets, each issue is openly debated with arguments for and against, until the vote is finally taken. When the vote is taken, a change comes over the situation. Once the vote is taken, the decision is unanimously binding on every

---

[2] Liu Shao-chi, *op. cit.*, p. 50.

member of the committee. Back they go to their local units to carry the verdict to them. They may not go back and say, "This is how the committee voted, but personally I was against it." They must present the verdict enthusiastically and with conviction. The decision of the district council is binding on every member of the local group. No decision can ever be appealed below. Under special circumstances it can be appealed to a higher committee.

In a similar fashion, the district committees elect representatives to a higher committee. The decisions of that higher committee, once made, are unanimously binding on every member, and binding everywhere below it, with a possibility of appeal above. Finally, the Central Committee of the Party is reached. From the Central Committee there is elected the executive of the Central Committee, known as the Presidium, formerly called the Politburo. With this committee the ultimate is reached. Since decisions made at each committee level are unanimously binding everywhere below it, decisions made by the top committee, the Presidium of the Central Committee, are absolute and final. There is no possibility of appeal. Their decisions carry the character of absolute truth.

The members of this Presidium are tried, proven Communists. They have worked their way up by hard, dedicated service. They are long established in the principles of Communist discipline and obedience and they observe unfalteringly the principle that the majority vote is final and absolute. Before the vote is taken, they may oppose a proposal vehemently, but once the vote is taken they must believe that the majority decision is right with their whole heart. No vestige of conscientious objection remains. As a united body they report to the Central Committee. The Central Committee hears the report, is instructed in the reasons for it, and unanimously approves it. From the Central Committee, the delegates go down to the next committee level where the same process is repeated. The report is given, unanimously approved, and processes to work it out are established. In this way, a decision reached at the top committee level becomes binding on every member throughout the entire organization.

Periodically, we see evidence of what appears to be fundamental division within the Communist Party. Leading Communists are suddenly hurled from their seats of power. They plunge into the abyss of shame, disgrace, and, frequently, of death. When we hear of quarreling in the top ranks of Communism, we smile happily and wait for the split to come, and for Communism to disintegrate. But our hopes are always doomed to disappointment because we do not understand that quarreling at the top level of Communism leading to the disgrace of leading Communists is not an evidence of division, but a proof of unity. It is not a manifestation of weakness; it is a sign of strength.

Historically, this is quite easy to prove. In 1924, Lenin died. He left the destiny of world Communism in the hands of a Politburo of seven men. All were Communist world figures, each of them utterly dedicated to the Communist cause. All of them had given a lifetime of service to Communism, had forsaken home, family, and fortune, had undergone hardship and suffered imprisonment and privation for the sake of Communism. When Lenin died, they turned on one another in an orgy of mutual destruction. When the final record was written, Stalin had emerged victorious and the other six had died violent deaths. According to our customary interpretation, the Communist Party should have been rent asunder and have shivered into fragments. In actual fact, the very reverse took place. It acquired a monolithic unity and strength, and went ahead to conquer well nigh half the world.

This seems incomprehensible because the principle of democratic centralism has not been understood. According to this principle, the decision of the Presidium is absolute. If that committee votes that one member is a traitor, he must believe that he is a traitor, he must confess that he is a traitor, and he must welcome his own execution. For his mind is the mind of the Party, and his life belongs to the Party. The willingness of the top Communist leadership to act in this way is an evidence of unity and strength, not of division and weakness. It reveals their total dedication and devotion to the Party.

When Lenin died, the great name in Communism was Leon Trotsky. The name of Trotsky was linked with that of Lenin throughout the chancelleries of the world as the author of the Communist revolution. Most people expected Trotsky to assume power. Trotsky was a great orator, a military genius, a brilliant philosopher, historian and author.

But Trotsky had joined the Bolsheviks only in 1917. He was more or less a "Johnnie come lately." In 1903, he had been called "the dagger of Lenin," and was Lenin's spokesman. In 1905, when revolution broke out in Russia, Trotsky was the chairman of the Petrograd Soviet. When the revolution failed he was arrested and brought to trial. He made a great oratorical defense of the right of revolution, but was convicted, and sentenced to lifetime Siberian exile. Czarist treatment of political prisoners was benign and compassionate compared with the treatment meted out by the Communists. He escaped shortly after he arrived in Siberia, and went into European exile.

Between 1905 and 1917 Lenin and Trotsky quarrelled constantly about points of doctrine. Lenin led the Bolsheviks; Martov led the Mensheviks; and Trotsky led an intermediate group trying to conciliate the Bolsheviks and the Mensheviks. Trotsky called Lenin the exploiter of the worst elements of the proletariat. Lenin called Trotsky a compromiser without principle.

Lenin returned to Russia in April, 1917, and formed the Communist Party from the Bolshevik segment of the Russian Social-Democratic Labor Party. Trotsky arrived in May from Nova Scotia, Canada, where he had been interned. He was met at the railway station by cheering throngs and made a speech in line with the policies of Lenin. In July, 1917, he joined the Bolsheviks. When the July revolution was a failure, Trotsky was arrested and Lenin went into hiding. However, influences were brought to bear for Trotsky's release. He was re-elected chairman of the Petrograd Soviet, and chairman of the Military Revolutionary Committee. As such he was official military head of the Communist revolution. Following the success of the revolution, he was

Foreign Minister and creator and Commander-in-Chief of the
Red Army. He was leader of the Red Army while it defeated the
armies of intervention. He was a member of the Politburo until
1924.

Trotsky had a great name and a great popular following. He
was a hero to the Red Army. But the fact that he had a great
name was unimportant. The fact that he was Commander-in-
Chief of the Red Army, and its idol, was also unimportant. The
only important thing was the vote he could get in the Politburo
of the Communist Party after Lenin's death. Trotsky received
practically no votes at all, for Zinoviev, Kamenev, and Stalin
formed a triumvirate to keep him out of power. The death of
Lenin was followed by an interregnum of collective leadership.
Trotsky was expelled from the Politburo, dismissed as Commander-in-Chief of the Red Army, and exiled from Russia. He
could have taken the Red Army and turned it against the Communist Party, but he refused to do so. The Communists have a
name for the act of using military power for political purposes.
They call it "Bonapartism." Trotsky scorned Bonapartism. He
said, "History has given one instrument only for the fulfillment of
its purpose. That instrument is the Communist Party." When he
was escorted to the Turkish border, he made them push him
across. He wanted it on record that he had not left Russia of his
own volition.

He settled eventually in Mexico City where he organized and
wrote. He formed the Fourth International. His name, meanwhile, had become the synonym of evil and hatred within the
Communist empire. The word "Trotskyite" was the vilest curse
word their tongues could find. Finally he was assassinated by a
young man who wormed his way into the Trotsky organization
and awaited his opportunity. When that moment came, he took
a short-handled ax, the kind used for mountain-climbing, and
crashed it through the skull and into the brain of Leon Trotsky.

Trotsky had the greatest reputation in Russia on the death of
Lenin. But Trotsky was voted out by the Politburo, and his fame
availed him nothing. According to the principle of democratic

centralism, the decision of the Politburo of the Communist Party is final and absolute.

The men who caused Trotsky's overthrow in the Politburo were Zinoviev, Kamenev, and Stalin. Zinoviev and Kamenev had been Lenin's lifelong collaborators and co-workers. They were brilliant writers with famous names. Zinoviev was in charge of the Leningrad Soviet organization and head of the Communist International. Kamenev was President of Soviet Russia. Stalin did not have the brilliance, the oratory, or the writing skill of the other two, but he was Secretary of the Politburo and the Party. As secretary, he was the man who appointed all the provincial officials. He was the bureaucrat par excellence. Suddenly, to their amazement, Zinoviev and Kamenev found themselves isolated in the Politburo. They were expelled from the Politburo, and from the Communist Party. They humbled themselves, confessed their sins, and pleaded for readmission to the Party as ordinary members. Their request was granted. Thus began the mad, recurring cycle of confession, expulsion, and readmission until, finally, in the great Stalinist purges of 1936, they stood up and said, "We are unfit to live. We have betrayed the working class. Please take us out and shoot us." Stalin hastened to grant their last request.

The rise of Stalin to complete power was unnoticed until accomplished. It was widely anticipated that the mantle of Lenin's power would finally rest on the capable shoulders of Nikolai Bukharin. Bukharin was a brilliant Communist theorist, author of *The A B C of Communism,* head of the Communist International after the decline of Zinoviev; a man of the caliber of Lenin himself. When the vote was taken, however, Stalin was victorious by a majority of four to three. Once the vote was taken it was binding on all seven members of the Politburo. Unanimously they went down to report the verdict to the Central Committee and, finally, the vote at the top became the belief and the marching orders of the entire Communist Party. There is no way whereby quarreling among the leadership can transfer itself to Party membership.

Stalin was then in complete power. He appointed those whom he approved. As secretary of the Politburo, he was in charge of the calling of the meetings and determined the agenda of those meetings. From 1929 until his death in 1953 his power remained absolute.

The rise of Stalin to personal and absolute dictatorship was not due to the qualities of his personality, but due to the nature of the structure of the Communist Party. An accepted Communist principle is that every member is subject to Party discipline. This is a euphemism for the reality that every member is under constant, personal, intimate supervision. The organized instrument to administer Party discipline was called the Orgburo. Associated with it was the internal Party police. Individuals rose to great heights of administrative power within the Communist Party, yet the secret police supervised their lives in minute detail. Their telephone calls were monitored. Their individual interviews were recorded. Their papers, both personal and public, were at the disposal of the secret police who possessed a key to the safe of every official. The only Communist official to whom this did not apply was the number one man, Joseph Stalin. To him the secret police finally reported and from him they took their orders.

Thus every member of the Politburo, powerful as he was, was isolated from all other members. There was no possibility of the prior consultation necessary if united and planned action was to be taken at a Politburo meeting. If two members should meet and Stalin should become suspicious, they could quickly be arrested and thus prevented from reaching the next meeting. In this way, each meeting of the Politburo was under the complete domination of Stalin. All other members in attendance were isolated from each other and the information on which their decisions were to be made was given to them by Stalin himself. In this manner his power became limitless.

His achievements are unbelievable. Khrushchev recounts them in detail in his speech attacking the cult of personality and outlining the "mistakes" of Stalin, but he does not clearly indicate

how Stalin did it. He tells us, for example, that Stalin put to
death the military leaders of Russia who were the idols of the
armed forces. He tells us that Stalin caused to be arrested and
shot for treason 70 per cent of the Central Committee that elected
him to power in 1934—98 members out of 137. He tells us of
entire nationalities that Stalin destroyed. He relates how, during the war, Stalin sat in an office with a globe in front of him
and gave specific orders to the military commanders in the field.
In one operation alone, because of the ignorance of Stalin and
his refusal to heed the plea of the commanders in the field, hundreds of thousands went to their deaths. Khrushchev tells us what
Stalin did, but he does not explain what gave him the power to
do it. How does a man put to death the majority of the military
commanders? How does he put to death the majority of the
leaders of his own political party?

Khrushchev gives an indication when he says, "Different members of the Politburo reacted in different ways at different times."
To understand this statement, we must understand the situation
that existed. The Politburo was made up of seven men, each of
them all-powerful within his administrative department, but
each of them under constant, hourly surveillance. The internal
Communist secret police checked everyone they met, listened in
on every phone conversation, had a key to every safe, read every
document, and reported everything they did to Stalin. Two of
them might desire to confer on some question to come before
the Politburo. They could not do it. If Stalin heard of their
meeting, he would have them arrested before the next session of
the Politburo was called. Thus each of them came to a Politburo
meeting completely unaware of the attitude of other members.
Not one of them had any idea how the others were going to vote.
If a man voted against Stalin and the motion was defeated, his
life was ultimately forfeit. This was the end result of the all-or-
nothing law of Communism. Only when this situation is clearly
visualized can we understand why the other members of the
Politburo were powerless to halt the cataract of Stalinist crimi-
nality. Only in the light of the understanding of Communist or-

ganization does the plaintive plea of Khrushchev, "Different members of the Politburo reacted in different ways at different times," become significant.

Stalin occupied a position of limitless power from which he operated as a tyrant unequalled in the annals of history. But it was Communism, not Stalin, that was responsible for his tremendous power. It was the organizational structure of Communism that projected him to his all-powerful position.

Communist organization remains the same. It has not changed. The events following the death of Stalin recapitulate minutely the events following the death of Lenin. Multitudes of people stand up and say, "Ah, but there is a difference! Stalin used to execute those he expelled, but Khrushchev does not." Such people have no knowledge of history. Lenin died in 1924. Stalin came to total power in 1929. The expellees from the Politburo were not executed until 1936. In the meantime, they were frequently given jobs appropriate to their abilities in distant areas. The same thing has happened since Stalin died. Immediately after the death of Stalin, there was a period of collective leadership followed by the emergence of Bulganin and Khrushchev. Bulganin was eventually overthrown and appointed to some minor position. Today at the top is the all-powerful Khrushchev, projected by the Communist Party to leadership of the Communist movement throughout the world.

Those who prate on the importance of public opinion within Russia, and proclaim the power of the Red Army, are ignorant of the political facts of life in Communist countries. All power resides in the Communist Party. Some time ago a name frequently in public discussion was that of Zhukov, Commander-in-Chief of the Red Army, friend of President Eisenhower. Our pundits advised that President Eisenhower and Zhukov meet and negotiate. They pointed out that the Red Army was a very powerful organization and claimed that Zhukov as its Commander-in-Chief was the real power in Russia. Let Zhukov and President Eisenhower get together and they could iron out the problems of the world.

In truth, Zhukov's position as Commander-in-Chief of the Red Army gave him no more power than if he had been head of the Boy Scouts. All power is in the Communist Party. The Communist Party is a unified, disciplined party. The man at the top has all authority. From its membership one disciplined man is taken and made Commander-in-Chief of the Red Army. In his administrative position within the army he is very powerful, but as a Communist he is totally subject to the orders that come down from the top of the Communist Party. Similarly, other men are selected to fill all significant governmental, educational, cultural and religious positions, but each of them owes complete obedience to the head of the Party.

The difference between the State and the Party is rarely understood. The head of the Russian State may be an insignificant individual When Stalin was all-powerful within Russia, while he was putting to death the majority of the officers of the Red Army, the majority of leading Communists, the majority of industrial managers, he was merely Secretary of the Communist Party. When it was necessary for him to meet with President Roosevelt in the capacity of chief of the Soviet State, he appointed himself to that position. When he thought it advisable, he appointed himself Commander-in-Chief of the Red Army. But his power never depended on his being President of Russia, or Commander-in-Chief of the Red Army. His power was derived from his position as head of the Communist Party.

For the Communist, the Party becomes the very voice and breath of God. The statement by Nikolai Bukharin before his execution is most revealing. Said he, "Comrades, I feel it is my duty to make the following statement. You all know that for three months I would say nothing. Suddenly I changed and confessed to everything of which I was accused by the Comrade Prosecutor. Why the change? I think you are entitled to know. As the moment of death approaches and one goes out into the great loneliness, the thought of going out alone, unforgiven, apart from the Party in which I have lived and which to me has been life itself, was a prospect I could not face; and, if by some miracle I should not die, life outside the Party would to me b ɔ worse than death itself." There is something frightening abou a movement that can evoke such devotion in one it is about tɔ destroy.

The curse of Communism is that by the Party it creates, it takes the idealism of its young recruits and uses it as an ultimate instrument of dictatorship, tyranny and genocide. Their intelligence is prostituted, their idealism debauched, and they are molded into intellectual robots of unquestioning obedience and frightening efficiency at the disposal of the dictator of the Party.

IV

THE COMMUNIST AT WORK—
Communist Fronts and Captive Organizations

THE COMMUNISTS have never aimed at the conversion of great masses of people to Communism. Their whole concept is that of a small party, compact, mobile, disciplined and dedicated, consisting largely of an intellectual elite. It is the task of this small group to utilize scientifically the social forces that move and direct the masses of the people so that the Communist Party may come to power over them, and impose forcibly the Communist program. The program of Communism, then, is to recruit into the service of the Party great numbers of individuals most of whom are unconscious that they are serving the Communist purpose.

Frequently it is asked, "How do you tell a Communist?" It is not always easy. If a Communist does not wish to reveal his Communist membership, it may be difficult indeed to establish the fact that he is a Communist. One test that may give valuable information could be called the "word test." There are certain words in rather common usage which mean one thing to people in general, and something entirely different to the Communists. If such a word is introduced into conversation, a person's position may be indicated by his interpretation of that word.

One such word for example, is "sectarian." To most people, this word is primarily associated with religion. To the Communist, however, it means quite another thing. The term "sectarian" would be applied to a Communist who publicly advocates Communism and thereby isolates himself, instead of joining an organization and working hard for its objectives so that he can finally use that organization for Communist purposes. Thus he multiplies his own power many times.

Lenin clearly discusses sectarianism in his remarkable book, *Left Wing Communism: an Infantile Disorder.* The book was written as a textbook to direct the Third International or Comintern which had been organized in 1919 to work for world revolution. It is directed primarily against a group of enthusiastic young German Communists. The position they took was that they were Communists and proud of it. They wanted the whole world to know. They disguised neither their objectives nor their methods. With their goal clearly in view they marched towards it, spurning compromise and deceit. Whatever the difficulty or danger, they neither turned nor flinched. They would die for Communism, but they would not co-operate with their enemies or compromise their principles.

Lenin turned upon these young enthusiasts, whom he called Left Wing Communists, the full power of his invective which both his friends and enemies acknowledge as considerable. Although he did not believe in God he said "God Himself has ordained that the young should be stupid." He ridiculed their unwillingness to indulge in compromise and deceit. He stated that they had accepted the limitations imposed by the bourgeois enemy. Compromise and deceit were very powerful instruments in the Communist program. He pointed out that a speaker openly advocating Communism was isolating himself from the great majority and limiting himself to a handful of rabid followers. True Communist strategy was to discover an issue that was important to a large number of people, to focus upon it, and to rally to it a large popular group. The test of their Communist caliber was the skill they showed in directing the people thus rallied into the service of the ultimate Communist purpose.

In illustration of this principle, Lenin gave specific instructions to members of the Communist Party of England to join the British Labour Party if they could, and to work for Henderson who was the Labour candidate for Prime Minister at that time. He said:

> At present the British Communists very often find it hard to approach the masses and even to get a hearing from them. If I come out as a Communist and call upon the workers to vote for Henderson against Lloyd George, they will certainly give me a hearing. And I will be able to explain in a popular manner not only why Soviets are better than parliament and why the dictatorship of the proletariat is better than the dictatorship of Churchill (disguised by the signboard of bourgeois "democracy"), but also that I want with my vote to support Henderson in the same way as the rope supports a hanged man.[1]

To be sectarian, then, is to operate in isolation instead of utilizing the great social forces that activate large groups of people. Sectarianism ranks high in the list of cardinal Communist sins.

The Communist formula for effective action is a simple one. It may be summed up: Discover what people want, promise it to them, and go to work to get it for them that you may come to power over them. This is the Communist program of action in any situation.

In Marxist schools the Communists study the groups that compose a given society. They study the emotions of each group, their longings and their grievances, and they devise a program to exploit these ambitions and resentments. They believe that each group of people is so short sighted and so selfishly motivated that, provided you are working in the interests of their most pressing desires in the immediate environment, they will pay no attention to what you are promising and promoting at a distance.

The Communist is not at all disturbed by the fact that he may be working simultaneously for two groups with conflicting in-

---

[1] V. I. Lenin, *"Left-Wing" Communism, an Infantile Disorder* (Moscow: Foreign Languages Publishing House, 1950) pp. 120-1.

terests and objectives. This is not inconsistency; it is the application of science.

The Communists have one objective—to come to power. They will do whatever is necessary for them to achieve this goal. In the economic realm, for example, they have no consistent economic program from country to country. Communist economic policy is to find out what any group wants and promise it to them. Classical Marxist economics advocated the collective ownership of land, but the Communists came to power in Russia and China by the reverse policy of the distribution of land, by making everybody a little Capitalist. Communist policy is to do whatever is necessary to advance the Communist Party's drive to dictatorial power.

Speaking at a girls' school in Dallas, Texas, I outlined to them the Communist formula for advance: Find out what people want, promise it to them, and go to work to get it for them in order to come to power over them. One girl asked the very natural question, "If the Communists promise people all sorts of things but do not fulfill their promises when they come to power, why are they not thrown out?" I replied, "If I get into this room by promising you girls that I have a lotion that will make each of you very beautiful, and if, as soon as I get in here, I pull out a machine gun and train it on you, why don't you throw me out?" Communism is, in essence, the technique of securing power by promising the immediate fulfilment of the dearest ambitions of the populace, and retaining power by the efficient use of force.

The Communists go to the working man and promise him higher wages, shorter working hours and better conditions generally. They approach the employer with the glittering prospect of industrial peace, good trading relations and higher profits. To the colored man they promise first-class citizenship. They will strive so that he may live where he wants to live, work where he wants to work, and marry whom he wants to marry. They promise the opponents of the Negro that they will keep the colored man where he belongs. To the Jew the vision they present is that they will end anti-Semitism for all time. To the Arab they vow that they will eliminate the Jews. They tell the Christian of glorious religious freedom and Christian revival under Communism. Their promise to the Hindu is to aid in the conversion of every Christian and Moslem to the Hindu religion. The Moslem is lured by the promise of assistance in promoting the cause of Islam.

Their program of deception is so often successful for two reasons. In the first place, as far as people can observe in the local situation, the Communists are sincere and keep their promises. It is a characteristic of Communist conduct to work hard and sacrificially for the immediate needs of the group they are endeavoring to exploit.

A Communist attorney will frequently accept a case without any charge, and will work tirelessly and effectively on behalf of his client in the courts of the land. To the individual and his friends he appears a true angel of mercy. They know nothing of the deeper motives that lie behind his conduct.

An example of the effective and apparently sincere assistance Communism can render to oppressed minorities comes from Italy. A missionary representing an evangelistic Protestant denomination came into conflict with the local authorities and was prevented from conducting his Sunday evening services. He was approached by the Communist leader of that city who sympathized with him in his predicament and claimed that it was a violation of the Italian constitution which granted freedom of religion.

To prove his sincerity he invited the missionary to utilize the facilities of the Communist Party headquarters to conduct his evening service. Thus the preacher stood on the platform provided by the Communist Party under the photograph of the benign and smiling Joseph Stalin and proclaimed the Christian gospel. It is easy to imagine how difficult it would be to convince such a man that Communism is incompatible with religious liberty. His own experience assures him that they are the great practical supporters of religious liberty. He is entirely oblivious to the fact that once Communism assumes power not only his liberty to preach but also his liberty to breathe would be in serious jeopardy.

In the second place, the local objective advanced by the Communists is frequently one which, taken in isolation, would merit support. They go to religious groups, for example, in the name of peace. They are ardent advocates of slum clearance and improved housing. Today they are the exponents of a puritanical morality in contrast to their position some time back.

In foreign countries, Christian missionaries teach the natives such Christian principles as "Thou shalt love they neighbor as thyself," and "Love your enemies." The Communist then approaches the mission convert with a program which seems to do nothing but advance the immediate well being of his neighbor and therefore merits his support as a Christian. He teams up with the Communist for this one purpose and the first step is taken on the bitter pathway of deviation and doom which Communism has marked out for his unwary feet.

A knowledge of the true program of Communism and its strategy and tactics is the only protection good people of every sort have against the Communist snare.

FRONTS

In order to involve as many people as possible, the Communists organize large numbers of Fronts, each of them designed to exploit the self-interest of a given group. Some of these are local and temporary, simple in formation and outline, and designed to exploit some local situation to the full. Others are on a world-wide scale with vast, permanent apparatus working year after year throughout the world. Whether large or small, the purpose of these Fronts is to recruit well-meaning people to serve unconsciously the Communist conspiracy.

The following experience illustrates rather well a simple Communist method of operation. After addressing a civic club one noon, I visited the Communist book store in Berkeley, California. It was called the Twentieth Century Bookstore and at that time was located outside the gate of the University of California. With me was a minister who was very well informed on the subject of Communist techniques.

One entire window of the store was given over to a display of booklets prepared by the Communists on behalf of a Negro called Wells. While serving a life sentence in San Quentin prison, Wells had thrown a cuspidor in the face of his guard and had smashed his face. Under Californian law, a prisoner serving a life sentence who uses violence against a guard is customarily condemned to death. The death sentence had been passed. Many people thought that the sentence was excessive.

The Communists saw in this situation a social force, an emotion common to a group of people which could be exploited for the Communist purpose. They set out to stir up agitation on behalf of Wells. After some months of agitation, they had prepared a book of some eighty or ninety pages showing what they had allegedly done on Wells' behalf. The book did not help Wells very much, but it presented the Communist Party in a very benign and humane light.

The minister who was with me took the book and started to browse through it. He had glanced through the Legal Committee for Justice for Wells, and was reading through the Religious Committee for Justice for Wells when he was startled to find there the name of a friend of his, the minister in whose church I was to speak that evening. He said, "Take this book out to him, tell him where you found it, and see what he has to say."

That evening we had a fine meeting. The minister was intelligent and patriotic. He was a fervent evangelical Christian and apparently an informed anti-Communist. Visiting after the meeting I produced the book, told him where I had found it, opened it, and showed him his name. His face fell. He said, "Fancy their doing that!"

"How did you come to get mixed up in this?" I asked.

"I didn't sign that the sentence be changed," he replied, "but only that it be reviewed."

"No you didn't," I said, and I read him the letter to which his signature was attached. "How did you become involved in it?"

He said, "A man said to me that here we had an example of cruelty and barbarity, and that as the Christian ministry was the servant of the forgiving and loving Christ, surely it was their duty to protest against the cruel, barbarous treatment of this man. If they did not protest, who would? He gave me the names of other ministers who were associated with this protest, and I thought it would not do any harm if I let my name go in too."

"What was the man's name?" I asked.

"He didn't tell me his name," was the reply.

"What did he look like?"

"I didn't see him."

"How did he get in touch with you?"

"He called me on the phone."

"Do you mean to tell me," I said, "that a man called you on the phone, and, without knowing who he was or what he represented, you allowed your name to go into an organization of this nature? Do you know what will happen? The Attorney General's Department, the House Un-American Activities Committee, or some official investigative agency will classify this movement as a Communist Front. Somebody will then observe your name and you will be classified as a supporter of Communist Fronts. What is more, the truth is that you are supporting a Communist Front. You did not do so willingly, but you have been outsmarted. They have exploited your basic Christian compassion for their purpose."

This is a regular Communist method of operating. Anybody not specifically informed about their methods could have been trapped in a similar fashion. It has happened to thousands. J.B. Matthews made the statement that seven thousand Protestant ministers in the United States have been involved in the Communist apparatus by allowing their names to be associated with some Communist Front. His statement was met with indignant and angry protests and treated as an attack on the Protestant ministery. There were a few honest ministers such as Daniel Poling of New York who humbly and courageously acknowledged the truth. Daniel Poling said, "As one of the seven thousand, I think the figure is far too low."

The principles according to which a Communist Front is organized can best be understood in terms of a series of concentric circles. At the center is the Communist Party, a small group whose members are organized, disciplined, and dedicated, and which has a single mind, will and purpose. This Party is composed of both open Communists such as William Z. Foster, Chairman of the American Communist Party, and crypto or hidden Communists, people who deny their Communist association and affiliation, but who are nevertheless dedicated Communists. The Communist Party is never entirely above ground. Clear rules to this effect were laid down in the by-laws of the Comintern where it is stated that in countries where a Communist Party is allowed legal existence, the legal party must be associated with an illegal party, and that the legal party must be under the control of the illegal party. The controlling segment of the Party is always underground.

Surrounding this small party at the center there is the zone of fellow travellers. A fellow traveller is one who approves Communist philosophy, Communist objectives, Communist organization and tactics, but who, for some personal reason, has not submitted himself to total Party discipline. He has never been able to reach the point of complete personal surrender necessary for actual Party membership. Fellow travellers frequently have guilty consciences because they are not Party members. They are subject in large measure to Party discipline, and they will willingly and sacrificially work with the Communists, but they can go into any court in the land, and swear under oath that they are not Communists because they are not members of the Party. Some of the prominent and powerful Americans who have served

Communism most faithfully have been fellow travellers. There is no evidence, for example, that Harry Dexter White, who betrayed American governmental secrets to the enemy and provided aid to the Communists in every possible way, was a Communist. He was a fellow traveller.

Surrounding the zone of fellow travellers is the zone of sympathizers. This zone contains different groups who are sympathetic to the Communist Party—various brands of Socialists, collaborators, and pacifists. Sympathizers are against certain features of Communism. They claim to be against the brutality of the Communists, as well as against their use of censorship and their denial of individual liberty. Nevertheless they believe that, on the whole, Communism has achieved many good things. While they cannot approve of Communism altogether, they feel that there are many good features about it, and that it is progressive and in the interests of the working class, and that it is possible to associate with the Communists in a local worthy objective. They feel that if they work with the Communists, are tolerant of them, and love them a little, they will win them from their extreme practices, and that the evil features of Communism will wither away leaving only that which is worthwhile. In the group there are a number of religionists who are particularly prone to argue in this way.

Surrounding the zone of sympathizers is the zone of pseudo-liberals. Most of these liberals are to be found in the ivory cloisters of colleges and universities, frequently occupying professorial chairs, and usually characterized by a pseudo-intellectual outlook. They take this attitude: "I am against Communism. I am against the Communist restraint of human liberty, I am against their censorship, I am against their dictatorship, and I am against their brutality. Nevertheless, I refuse to become like my enemies in order to oppose them, and while I hate what the Communists say and do, I will fight for the rights of the Communists to speak and organize even as I will fight for my own rights." Thus in effect, they become the protectors and the runners of interference for the Communist conspirators. They uphold the right of Communists to be professors in schools and universities. They are the great defenders of the Fifth Amendment. They contend that no restraint or restriction of any kind should be applied to an individual because he has availed himself of the Fifth Amendment. Apparently their viewpoint is that nobody should suffer any social restraints or disadvantages unless there is evidence that is valid in a court of law.

Their argument is fallacious because they project certain conditions which prevail in the realm of law into the realm of privilege and social activity where they do not apply. For example, a man approaches the president of a bank seeking employment. The president, however, has heard a rumor that he was dismissed from his last employment because he had embezzled funds, and asks the man if this is true. The man refuses to answer on the grounds that he might incriminate himself. The man is quite within his rights in refusing to incriminate himself, and certainly cannot be sent to prison because of his reply, but if the bank president were to employ that man, he would be foolish indeed. The Fifth Amendment refers merely to imprisonment and legal penalty. Any attempt to project it beyond that realm is not intellectualism or liberalism, but stupidity.

The following little fantasy which I have called "The Liberal's Dilemma" outlines the position reached when it is claimed that no restraints can be placed on anyone in any situation unless there is evidence that is valid in a court of law, and that the Fifth Amendment carries no implication of guilt.

THE LIBERAL'S DILEMMA

Motherhood is gathered in its beauty and its purity, desperately concerned because of the increase in juvenile delinquency due to the prevalence of organized vice in the district. So widespread is juvenile delinquency becoming that the very foundation of the family itself is in danger. The mothers are determined that something must be done to eliminate organized vice.

It is decided to form a Committee of Maternal Purity. The meeting is called, and a woman of great liberal outlook is installed as temporary chairman. She calls for nominations from the floor for the position of permanent chairman of the committee. To everybody's astonishment, the name of Madame Vice, madame of the local brothel, is nominated for the position. The chairman looks startled, then says, "I hear the name of Madame Vice nominated for the position of chairman of our Committee of Maternal Purity. Does anyone wish to speak on this motion?"

An indignant voice cries out, "But that's ridiculous! She's the cause of most of the trouble! She's a prostitute and a keeper of a house of prostitution."

"These are serious charges," the chairman says. "They must be supported by unimpeachable evidence. Anybody who can rise and say that they have first hand evidence that this woman has indulged in these alleged practices, please rise and speak."

Nobody moves.

The chairman says, "Since there is no evidence, apparently, to support these charges, I'll ask the woman herself. Madame, are you, as alleged, a prostitute and a keeper of a house of prostitution?"

The fur clad figure indignantly rises, "I ain't going to answer that question! You have no right to ask it! I ain't going to incriminate myself."

"Yes," says the chairman, "that is your privilege. Certainly no inference can be taken from that reply. There is no evidence to support these charges. From the woman's own words we can get no indication of their truth or falsehood. I have but one last recourse. Has this woman been indicted and convicted in a court of law?"

Silence again prevails, and the voice of liberal learning, rich and mellow, is heard. "I accept the nomination of Madame Vice as the Chairman of the Committee of Maternal Purity of this city."

By the same process, it is easy to conceive the election of Al Capone as Chairman of the Committee for Public Security of the Chicago of 1930. Such ridiculous situations become possible when a provision of the Constitution designed solely to grant immunity from legal punishment is projected into the realm of normal life which involves privilege and responsibility far removed from legal punishment. This is the error which is made by the pseudo-liberals who fail to see the basic malignancy of Communism and thus become a zone of protection behind which the Communist conspirators pursue their evil schemes.

Surrounding the zone of pseudo-liberals is the zone of dupes. In this zone are to be found the genuinely patriotic American citizens from a great variety of walks of life. They have simply been deceived. Many solid citizens are astonished when they discover the trap into which they have fallen.

Consider the hypothetical case of a successful businessman whose name appears on the letterhead of a Communist Front. He is whole-heartedly against Communism but is also exceedingly busy. He wishes to help good causes and will support them financially and with the use of his name. However, it must be remembered that he has many pressing demands upon his time and he cannot attend meetings or participate in the day to day activities of the organization. That task he must leave to others. In this manner, the Communists have successfully utilized the money and the prestige of many of their most fervent opponents.

THE BIRTH OF A FRONT

The essential purpose of the Communist Front must be camouflaged with an alleged purpose of wide popular appeal. The Communists are very well aware of what the true objective is, while most of the Front members see only the camouflage. A permanent Communist objective is to shift the balance of world military power in favor of Communist military strength. Wherever they can weaken the military strength of any free country, they help to achieve this purpose. One basic objective, then, is to weaken militarily all those countries opposed to Communism. Obviously if that real objective were proclaimed, it would not recruit many people in those countries. An organization which had the announced purpose of weakening America militarily so that Communist conquest would be easier would rally few supporters. Therefore there must be an announced objective which will accomplish the same purpose, but which will present itself in a totally different guise. One announced purpose could be the preservation of peace in the face of the possible horrors of a thermo-nuclear war. This is the basis of the array of unholy peace movements spawned by Communism.

Communist personnel are allotted to set up the organization of the Front. They enlist a few fellow travellers and together they decide the precise nature of the organization to be formed. The purposes are clearly designated, the basic executive officers are selected, mostly from the ranks of Communists or fellow travellers, and the slogans which are to recruit the people are formulated. When these preparations have been made, the fellow traveller approaches the sympathizer. The Communist himself does not customarily approach the sympathizer, for the sympathizer has certain qualms about the Communists. He knows that they cannot always be trusted. But the fellow traveller is able to assure him that he is not a Communist, and thus can make the approach with every hope of success.

He outlines to the sympathizer the objective, namely, the preservation of peace in the face of the desperate threat of war and annihilation that hangs over us all. He describes the demands for disarmament which are to be made, to Communist and non-Communist countries alike. He does not point out, of course, that these demands cannot possibly have any effect in Communist countries because there is no public opinion there that they can influence, and that the people of the Communist countries cannot even find out about these demands unless the Communist Party decides to tell them. He does not indicate that the real purpose

is to influence public opinion in free countries where the government is elected and controlled by the people. The sympathizer,
satisfied when these demands are nominally extended to all
countries, is sold on this magnificent idea and is enlisted in the
cause.

The sympathizer then approaches the pseudo-liberal who
thinks it a wonderful idea. He would not be happy to participate in a Communist plan, but he knows the sympathizer is not a
Communist. He is aware, maybe, that the sympathizer has some
radical ideas, but he, unlike most other people, is open-minded,
and does not hold that against him. Obviously the idea is an
excellent one and merits his support. Thus the pseudo-liberal
becomes the spokesman who approaches the dupe, the patriotic
businessman who will supply the finance and the respectability.
At the periphery, then, the patriotic businessman is approached
by an anti-Communist liberal for a worthy objective. The money
is provided, names are written on the letterhead, a public relations department is established, the propaganda is proclaimed,
and the organized Communist Front goes into operation. Superficially, it appears to be the work of patriotic businessmen, educators, scientists and others of repute, but behind these dupes
are the pseudo-liberals; behind them are the sympathizers; and
behind the sympathizers, at the very center, are the unseen Communists and fellow travellers who are in control of policy and
program.

Fronts such as this have been formed a thousand times and in
a thousand ways. They have recruited many well-meaning anti-
Communists into the service of Communism. Thus is Communist
science applied whereby the organized few multiply their effectiveness by organizing a mass movement that, on specific issues,
can sometimes make and break democratic, anti-Communist governments. Again the conclusion is clear that an understanding
mind and an alert attitude is the only protection the individual
has against involuntary involvement. Eternal vigilance is the
price of liberty.

CAPTIVE ORGANIZATIONS

Communist Fronts have been organized to exploit labor, religion, art, civil liberties, culture and nationalism. The Fronts that proclaim Peace and National Liberation have been particularly effective. In addition to these specially organized Fronts, the Communists make use of organizations that have been in existence for long periods. Frequently, these organizations were formed by non-Communists for non-Communist purposes, but nonetheless they become captives of Communism. This is made possible by the Communists' willingness to work hard at unpleasant tasks in the interests of such organizations. In every organization, there is a certain amount of routine work to be done, work that is not spectacular or interesting, and therefore not very appealing to most people. When the Communists join the organization, they work hard. They are available for dull and menial tasks. They write the letters, they wrap the packages, they prepare the mimeographed materials. Very often they are the finest workers that the organization has. When election time comes round, nothing is more natural than that they should be elected to executive office. Thus the Communists, by reason of their clarity of purpose, their drive towards an objective, and their hard, dedicated work, take over institutions that have been created with the money of Capitalist enterprise and use them to destroy liberty.

The Communists are magnificently organized. They have dedicated personnel and they have acquired vast experience. Only on a basis of understanding, organization and dedication can we hope to meet and defeat them. To hate them is futile. Some of their most effective servants have been their bitterest enemies. Eyes that see and minds that think must merge with hearts that love freedom, to meet this challenge.

V

TECHNIQUES FOR SEIZING POWER—
Philosophy of Violence

THE COMMUNISTS have worked out both theoretical and practical techniques for the achievement of their goal of world conquest. One of their fundamental theoretical texts is Lenin's book, *The State and the Revolution* which has now become the world's most translated book.

Lenin was in the process of writing this book when he left Switzerland to return to Russia in 1917 to organize the Communist seizure of power. The revolution that overthrew the Russian Czar in February, 1917, was not a Communist revolution, but a spontaneous mass rising supported by many different groups of people. When this genuine revolution took place, most of the important Communist personalities were in exile either in Siberia or in countries outside Russia. Once the revolution was accomplished, a political amnesty was declared. Thereupon, Bolsheviks and revolutionaries who had been scattered throughout the world converged on Petrograd. Stalin returned from exile in Siberia to assume editorship of the Communist Party paper, *Pravda*. Trotsky returned from Nova Scotia. Lenin returned from Geneva, Switzerland, where his pen had been pouring forth a floodtide of literature urging civil war in Russia. Upon his arrival in Petrograd, he informed the revolutionary workers that he had returned to conquer and govern Russia. His claim caused considerable astonishment, particularly in the ranks of the orthodox Marxists. It must be remembered that the Bolsheviks of whom Lenin was leader were but a small party numbering some twenty thousand members. Lenin's Marxist critics, when they heard his claim, said, "Farewell, Lenin the Marxist; welcome, Lenin the anarchist!"

Nonetheless, Lenin achieved the impossible. Within six months, with a small band of faithful followers, he had stolen the legitimate fruits of the revolution, betrayed the working people of Russia, and established the greatest tyranny and dictatorship the world has ever known. *The State and the Revolution* which he was writing at that time is still considered a fundamental theoretical textbook. In it Lenin sets forth how the Communists are to come to power within the state, and what they must do once they are in power.

Lenin here concentrates upon the necessity of violence. He considers government the instrument by which the ruling class controls and exploits the subject class. All government is class government, and the institutions of a state such as the legislature, the executive, the judiciary, the police power, the tax power, and the educational institutions, are the instruments of the ruling class for the exploitation of the subjective class. According to Lenin's thesis, the governments of Europe and America were bourgeois governments which existed to exploit the people. These governments could be overthrown only through violence and bloodshed.

To Lenin the use of force and violence was not to be merely a reaction to force and violence used by the Capitalists. To him force was an instrument of positive purpose and he was totally devoid of any apologetic attitude towards its use. He states categorically that violence is essential to their purpose: "The supersession of the bourgeois state by the proletarian state is impossible without a violent revolution." [1]

---

[1] V. I. Lenin, *The State and Revolution* (Moscow: Foreign Languages Publishing House), p. 35.

In saying this, Lenin went further than his mentor, Karl Marx, had done. Marx had allowed the possibility of bloodless revolutions in England and America. Marx claimed that since the bureaucracy was not developed to the same extent in these countries as in other European countries, and since the police and military power of these states was not so great, there existed the possibility of a peaceful transition to Socialism. Lenin said that these conditions no longer applied. In Europe, in England, and in America, the revolution to bring about the transition from the bourgeois state to the proletarian must be violent. There could be no possibility of non-violent, successful revolution.

One of the specific crimes for which Lenin mercilessly chastized Karl Kautsky, the leading Marxist theorist of the Second International, was his continued clinging to the possibility of a peaceful transition to Socialism in England and America as had been admitted by Marx. In his tirade, *The Proletarian Revolution and the Renegade Kautsky*, Lenin writes:

> Further, was there in the seventies anything which made England and America exceptional in regard to what we are now discussing? It will be obvious to anyone at all familiar with the requirements of science in regard to the problems of history that this question must be put. To fail to put it is tantamount to falsifying science, to engaging in sophistry. And, the question having been put, there can be no doubt as to the reply: the revolutionary dictatorship of the proletariat is violence against the bourgeoisie; and the necessity of such violence is particularly created, as Marx and Engels have repeatedly explained in detail (especially in "The Civil War in France" and in the preface to it), by the existence of a military clique and a bureaucracy. But it is precisely these institutions that were non-existent precisely in England and in America and precisely in the 1870's, when Marx made his observations (they do exist in England and in America now)![2]

The Communist attitude on violence is frequently misunderstood. Even the opponents of Communism think that the Communists do not necessarily want violence, that they use violence only because the exploiting class resists their assumption of

---

[2] V. I. Lenin, *The Proletarian Revolution and the Renegade Kautsky* (Moscow: Foreign Languages Publishing House, 1952), pp. 23-4.

power. This was never the viewpoint of the Communist leaders, particularly Lenin and Engels. Kautsky, who was reputed to have learned the entire works of Marx by heart, was viciously attacked by Lenin for his lukewarm attitude toward violence. Kautsky's attitude was that they might have to use violence but that if they had to do so it would be regrettable, for violence was bad and corrupted those who used it. In reply Lenin quoted from Engels' book, *Anti Dühring*:

> . . . That force, however, plays also another role (other than that of a diabolical power) in history, a revolutionary role; that, in the words of Marx, it is the midwife of every old society which is pregnant with a new one, that it is the instrument with the aid of which social movement forces its way through and shatters the dead, fossilized political forms—of this there is not a word in Herr Dühring. It is only with sighs and groans that he admits the possibility that force will perhaps be necessary for the overthrow of the economic system of exploitation—unfortunately, because all use of force, forsooth, demoralizes the person who uses it. And this in spite of the immense moral and spiritual impetus which has been given by every victorious revolution! And this in Germany, where a violent collision—which indeed may be forced on the people—would at least have the advantage of wiping out the servility which has permeated the national consciousness as a result of the humiliation of the Thirty Years' War. And this parson's mode of thought—lifeless, insipid and impotent—claims the right to impose itself on the most revolutionary party that history has known.[3]

Lenin was an enthusiastic advocate of violence. His revolution was to be no peaceful transition. It is possible to sense the delight with which he proclaimed Engels' teaching on this subject:

> Have these gentlemen (the anti authoritarians) ever seen a revolution? A revolution is certainly the most authoritarian thing there is; it is the act whereby one part of the population imposes its will upon the other part by means of rifles, bayonets and cannon—authoritarian means, if such there be at all; and if the victorious party does not want to have fought in vain, it must maintain this rule by means of the terror which its arms inspire in the reactionaries. Would the Paris Commune have lasted a single day if it had not made use of this authority of the armed

---

[3] Quoted by Lenin in *The State and Revolution*, pp. 32-3.

people against the bourgeois? Should we not, on the contrary, reproach it for not having used it freely enough? [4]

The second feature of the revolution described by Lenin in *The State and Revolution* was its purpose. The purpose of the revolution was not to seize control of the State, but to destroy it. Most of the book is given over to the thesis that the State must be destroyed. The State functions in many ways. It functions through the constitution; it functions through the executive authority—the President, the Cabinet, the Justice Department, the Police Department, the Defense Department; it functions through the legislature, through the judiciary, and through the civil service. The goal of Communism was not to secure a president exercising constitutional power. It was not to appoint the cabinet officers such as the Secretary of State or Defense. The appointment of the judges was not their avowed objective. The purpose was to destroy utterly the constitution, the legislative system, the judicial system, and the administrative system, to wipe out the State and build a new one in a totally different form.

Lenin's argument is based on Marx's analysis of what had happened in the French Commune in 1871 when the Communards tried to take over the Capitalist State and use it as an instrument of government. The Commune was soon overthrown. Lenin said that when a State is allowed to continue, it inevitably carries within itself the seeds of counter revolution. Its members have their vested interests in the old society. The State must be destroyed. This was expressed by William Z. Foster, Chairman of the Communist Party of America in his statement:

> No Communist, no matter how many votes he should secure in a national election, could, even if he would, become President of the present government. When a Communist heads a government in the United States—and that day will come just as surely as the sun rises—that government will not be a capitalistic government but a Soviet government, and behind this government will stand the Red Army to enforce the Dictatorship of the Proletariat.

---

[4] Quoted by Lenin in *The Proletarian Revolution and the Renegade Kautsky,* p. 27.

SEIZURE OF POWER

The assumption of power, then, is by violent revolution leading to the destruction of the State and the establishment of the
dictatorship of the proletariat. The Communists worked out
theoretical processes by which this seizure of power was to be
realized. History now records the practical methods by which
they have seized power in a number of countries, specifically,
Russia, China, and the misnamed People's Democracies of Eastern Europe.

The assumption of power may be by various methods of
which three will be discussed. They are:

1. Internal revolt through control of the labor unions
2. Military conquest
3. Piecemeal surrender to military blackmail.

REVOLT THROUGH LABOR UNION CONTROL ..

This traditional method which the Communists have advocated for many years has not as yet succeeded in the establishment of effective Communist power in any country. Originally
they saw the labor unions as the instrument through which the
Communist Party was to come to power. The program was as
follows. The Communists were to infiltrate the labor unions and
secure executive power within them. They were then to call an
industrial strike. This industrial strike would become a political
strike, then a general strike and finally a revolutionary strike
leading to armed insurrection and the conquest of power.

The first necessity was to infiltrate the labor unions. Lenin
specifically states this in his book, *"Left-Wing" Communism, an
Infantile Disorder.* How they got into the labor unions did not
matter. They were to work their way in, lie their way in, or buy
their way in. The all important thing was that they get in.

We must be able to withstand all this, (i.e. insults and persecution), to agree to all and every sacrifice, and even—if need be —to resort to various stratagems, artifices, illegal methods, to evasions and subterfuges, only so as to get into the trade unions, to remain in them, and to carry on Communist work within them at all costs.[5]

Industrial Strike

Once in power, at the appropriate moment, they were to call an industrial strike. An industrial strike is defined as one directed at the achievement of an industrial goal such as higher wages or shorter working hours. Generally speaking, such a strike can always be called. There are always grievances, and desires for improved conditions that any intelligent Communist leader can exploit. Moreover, an industrial strike is, generally speaking, the only type of strike which can be organized and maintained with the support of the workers. The industrial strike must then be transformed into a political strike.

Political Strike

A political strike is not designed to secure immediate, tangible, industrial benefits for the workers, but to destroy the Capitalist system. A political strike is designed to undermine the foundations of authority by creating chaos, unemployment, bitterness, hunger and fear. Usually, a political strike, as such, cannot be called, but an industrial strike can be transformed into a political one. As the political strike extends and grows into a general strike, many situations will arise where the striking workers come into conflict with organized authority, usually with the police, but sometimes with the military forces.

---

[5] V. I. Lenin, *"Left-Wing" Communism, an Infantile Disorder* (Moscow: Foreign Languages Publishing House, 1950), p. 65. (Words in parenthesis added.)

Revolutionary Strike

As acts of violence come to be associated with it, the political strike transforms itself into a revolutionary strike. When the revolutionary strike has developed sufficiently and drawn into its orbit enough working people, a general insurrection can take place. Thus the revolutionary strike transforms itself into armed insurrection. If the insurrection is successful, the Communists, through their control of the labor unions, will be able to establish their dictatorship of the proletariat.

This method, their traditional method for the seizure of power, has not yet brought them success in any country. But it has been a most important adjunct to their seizure of power and rehearsals of the process have taken place in many countries.

The last great strike wave organized by the Communists for this purpose was in the year 1949. During that year there were world-wide, co-ordinated, organized strikes. There was a dock workers' strike in England when the British authorities expelled from Britain as an international Communist agent Louis Goldblatt, secretary-treasurer of the International Longshore Workers and Warehousemen's Union. The islands of Hawaii approached economic strangulation during a dockworkers' strike that year. In Australia there was a coal-miners' strike. These strikes were co-ordinated on a world-wide scale.

The coal-miners' strike in Australia is of special interest as it was a rehearsal of the Communist program for the assumption of total power. In Australia, the Communist Party is an open political party and nominates candidates for political office in federal, state, and municipal government. These nominations are made in the name of the Communist Party. But the Communists in Australia have always been a small, politically insignificant minority, and their candidates invariably fail miserably. There is a system in Australia whereby a candidate, when he nominates for an elective office, must pay a deposit which is refunded if he secures a certain percentage of the votes of the leading candidate. This is designed to prevent frivolous candidates with no prospect of victory from swamping the candidate list. It is a great day for the Communist Party if one of their candidates saves his deposit. The Communists in Australia do not get elected to political office.

However, their industrial power is very strong indeed. By following Lenin's technique, this handful of Communists has come to power in a vast segment of Australia's labor unions. They are very hard workers, they are good organizers, and they are dedicated. Because of their organizing ability and dedication, they are frequently elected to executive union office.

When I was a resident medical officer in the General Hospital in Brisbane, Australia, the largest hospital in the Southern Hemisphere, the labor situation was most interesting. The official union of the non-medical workers at the Brisbane General Hospital was the Australian Workers' Union which, in its leadership, was fervently anti-Communist. The representative of the workers at the hospital was a man called King who was a fanatical Communist. King was elected by the workers as their representative in the hospital not because he was a Communist, but because he was prepared to work for them assiduously and courageously. Every day when they received their pay checks, King stood at the office and waited. If one of them had a grievance, he went to King who immediately went to the management. There he yelled and shouted if necessary, in order to have the supposed wrong righted. Those workers knew that if they had a grievance, King would be on their side, right or wrong, and that they could depend on him. Therefore, they made him their representative. The union itself was fanatically anti-Communist in its leadership and in its official publication. But local Communists such as King were able by sheer hard work to exercise considerable influence and authority. The workers served by such men saw only the dedication, not the ultimate purpose.

By this method the Communists were able to come to power in a large number of Australian unions. These unions included the Seamen's Union of Australia, the secretary of which was a fervent, self-proclaimed Communist, the Waterside Workers' Federation of which the secretary, Jim Healy, was a prominent Communist, and the Coal Miners' Federation which was under effective Communist control. In 1949, the steelworkers' union of Australia, known as the Federated Ironworkers' Union, was directed by Communist officials, though these have since been expelled. Thus the Communists were in considerable power in a very significant section of organized labor in Australia.

In the winter of 1949, a strike was called in the coal mining industry. Coal is the life blood of Australia. The country has no natural petroleum and no natural gas. Coal is the source of gas, electricity, and, basically, the source of transportation. It is the economic life blood of the country. This was particularly true in 1949. There had been a severe coal shortage since the end of the war. There were no coal stocks at grass anywhere in Australia. Coal that was mined one day was transported for use the following day. The coal that is used to provide gas for heating and cooking in Sydney comes from Newcastle which is one hundred miles to the north. If a storm was raging and a coal ship was held up, it was quite common for gas rationing to be imposed till the coal arrived. Public utilities and industry generally operated under the constant threat of coal starvation.

In this situation a coal strike was called. It was called in defiance of the established lawful processes for the settling of disputes, while the dispute was still before the arbitration authorities. It was called as an industrial strike demanding increased wages and fringe benefits.

When the strike began, chaos became the order of the day. There was immediate rationing of gas and electricity. Industries that depended upon electricity had to close down. Hundreds of thousands of men were thrown out of work. It was illegal to burn more than one electric light bulb in a home at any one time. Gas was allowed for an hour in the morning and an hour in the evening for cooking purposes only. It was mid-winter. Gas fires and electric radiators, which provide the only heat in most Australian homes, were prohibited without a medical prescription.

There were a number of tragedies. Old age pensioners, living in rooms by themselves and feeling desperately cold, would illegally light their gas fires and go to sleep. As they slept, the gas would be turned off at the main. Later the gas would be turned on again and flood their rooms with deadly fumes while they slept on. Many did not awaken.

The government in power at that time was the Australian Labour Party, an avowed, self-proclaimed Socialist Party. They declared that this was a revolutionary assault upon the authority and economy of the country and introduced drastic legislation. They sent the armed forces into the strip coal mines to mine coal for the people. They froze labor union funds retrospectively. The Waterside Workers' Federation, the Miners' Federation, and the Steel Workers' Union under Communist leadership had withdrawn large sums of money from the bank to use as strike pay. The executive officers of these unions were taken before the courts and ordered to produce these sums of money which they had withdrawn before the law freezing their funds was introduced. When they refused, they were sentenced to imprisonment for contempt of court.

Chaos developed. Everywhere there was strife and bitterness. The unemployed and the cold were ripe for Communist agitation. The Communist agitators placed the whole blame on the Capitalist system urging its overthrow.

There was a rehearsal for the armed insurrection. When Jim Healy, the secretary of the Waterside Workers' Federation, was sent to prison for refusal to obey the court's order to produce the money which had been withdrawn from the bank, the Communists agitated on the waterfront. They gathered the longshoremen together and told them that this was an assault on them. This man was their representative. They had elected him. It was their duty to stand by him. If they let this go without protest, soon more serious measures would be taken against them such as reductions in wages. The men were stirred up and, thousands strong, they marched through the streets. It did not break out into open violence, but all the potentials were there. If the moment had been considered ripe, an incident could have been started, leading to fighting. In this way a political strike becomes a revolutionary strike, and a revolutionary strike becomes armed insurrection.

The most revealing aspect of the whole situation was the helplessness of the workers and the power of the leaders in the crisis hours. Every labor union in Australia lined up, not in terms of the patriotism of its membership, but in terms of the Communist affiliation of its leaders. The membership of the unions was helpless while the leadership was all-powerful. This was very well illustrated by the different behavior of the railwaymen in the states of Victoria and New South Wales. Victoria and New South Wales, the two most populous Australian states, are contiguous to each other. There is no possible way by which you could differentiate the Victorian workers from those in New South Wales. They are similar in every respect. Nevertheless, the Victorian railwaymen were part of the Communist revolutionary front. They sided with the strikers and refused to move the coal mined by the army, declaring it hot. The railwaymen of New South Wales, on the other hand, handled the coal, transported it, and delivered it to public utilities, thus playing a large part in the maintenance of essential services. The railwaymen of New South Wales effectively thwarted the Communist objective of a transport strike to advance the revolution.

There was one all important difference between the railwaymen of the two states. In Victoria, the secretary of the railwaymen was Jack Brown, a Communist, while the secretary in New South Wales was Jack Ferguson, an anti-Communist. That was the sole difference, but in the crisis hour, these men had legal authority to make decisions which were binding on thousands of other men. The executives had the power to make the decisions unless a mass meeting was called to overthrow them. This was well nigh impossible since mass meetings may require up to fourteen days' notice. Multitudes may starve in fourteen days.

Frequently the argument is made that, provided that workers are patriotic, a few extreme union leaders do not matter very much. History has proven this to be nonsense. The International Longshore and Warehouse Workers' Union of the West Coast of the United States was expelled from the CIO because it was a consistent instrument of the international Communist conspiracy. The longshore workers of California are no less patriotic than the longshore workers of the East Coast, but on the West Coast they are controlled by a handful of Communist officials.

That the I.L.W.U. is slavishly devoted to Communist purposes is revealed in the published report of the Subcommittee to Investigate the Administration of the Internal Security Act and Other Internal Security Laws to the Committee on the Judiciary, United States Senate. This report reveals that during the collective or popular front period of the Communist Party, the I.L.W.U. supported Roosevelt's anti-aggression program. With the signing of the Stalin-Hitler pact, however, the I.L.W.U. suddenly discovered that the war in Europe was of no concern to it. It attacked President Roosevelt and his policy of giving aid to the allies. Following the opening of hostilities between Germany and Russia in June, 1941, the I.L.W.U. leadership reversed its policy and declared that the war in Europe was, after all, of vital concern to the labor movement. In the summer of 1944, Bridges and the I.L.W.U. executive board urged that the no strike pledge be extended into peacetime. With the end of the war in Europe and the collapse of the wartime collaboration between the Soviet Union and the Democratic Nations, the position of the I.L.W.U., like that of the Communist Party, underwent another change, and the no strike pledge was forgotten.

When the Truman Plan for Greece and Turkey was announced in the spring of 1947, it was bitterly attacked in the newspaper of the I.L.W.U., *The Despatcher*. In a front page editorial, it was compared with the international gangsterism of Hitler. When the Marshal Plan was enunciated, it too was condemned by the I.L.W.U. The I.L.W.U. has demanded that the United States cease testing and producing the atomic bomb without calling for international inspection of the Soviet's production of atomic weapons. The I.L.W.U. has opposed the North Atlantic Alliance. In June, 1949, *The Despatcher* hailed the liberation of China, comparing it with the American and French Revolutions. Thus thousands of men follow in minute detail every twist in the Communist Party line, because they are helpless in the hands of a few Communist leaders who control and direct their assets and utilize them for the Communist purpose.

A sample of this Communist process for the seizure of power has occurred here in America. It took place in San Francisco in 1934. Sam Darcy, former district organizer of the Communist Party of California, outlined the Party's plan of operation in his article on the San Francisco Bay area general strike in *The Communist* for October, 1934. The substance of the article was later presented in a report by Darcy to the seventh congress of the Communist International meeting in Moscow in August, 1935. The report reads as follows:

"Let me state here that there would have been no maritime or general strike except for the work of our party. The very fact that it was a sympathy strike gives it its political character. The fight began in the decisive sector of San Francisco's economy, namely, the maritime industry. It is apparent from the stated facts that the strike had a definite political character.

"About a week previous (to June 18), in anticipation of the possible needs for a general strike, we had succeeded in convincing the Painters Local 1158 to sign a circular letter addressed to all other locals of the A.F. of L., declaring their own support for a general strike, and asking their vote for it, so that, should a general strike become necessary, it would be possible to call it at the critical moment without any harmful delay.

"The very next day the Machinists Local 68, the oldest, and very influential A.F. of L. local in San Francisco voted to join the general strike movement.

"Of course, the general strike movement was in no sense a spontaneous movement. It took long and careful preparations. At first the militants (i.e. the Communists) sent small committees, chiefly from the longshoremen's local, to other A.F. of L. locals, appealing for support by a vote for a general strike. First we tackled only those locals that we knew were most militant. As we began to tackle the larger locals and those in the key industries which would be critical for the outcome of the general strike, we sent, not small delegations, but delegations ranging from fifty to as much as four hundred. The general strike movement was actually advancing very rapidly, by the votes which were daily taking place in the local unions stimulated largely by the delegations of militants.

"Yet the workers in the Longshoremen's local, an A.F. of L. affiliate and a craft union, were able under the pressure of circumstances, quickly to break down their own routine work inside their own local, and reach out to other locals as far removed from longshore work as bakers and cleaners and dyers, and help organize them for the general strike. Our strategy was to use the Joint Maritime Strike Committee as a base.

"On July 5 the National Guard took control of the waterfront. On that day finally, the Joint Maritime Strike Committee issued a leaflet openly calling for the general strike.

"Getting the Teamsters to join the strike was at this time the main force needed to make certain the eventuality of the general strike. This was due to the prestige and strategic post which the Teamsters had. On the night of the 11th the Teamsters met. This was, in a sense, a point which was decisive for the general strike. The Teamsters demanded to hear Bridges, who was given a tremendous ovation, and they finally voted to go out the next morning.

"By the next morning, July 12, 60 local unions had voted for the general strike and about 10 locals were already out.

"Saturday and Sunday were used by the militants for two activities, first, to pull the remaining locals out, and, secondly, to mobilize for organizational contact. We had to develop a movement within all the local unions, for special membership meetings to elect the five to the General Strike Committee instead of appointing them. The militants also tried through agitation, such as a leaflet issued by the Longshoremen's local, a statement by Harry Bridges, an appeal by the party and the Western Worker, etc., to stimulate the workers to force the election of the delegations of five to the General Strike Committee in their locals. We tried to get an appeal from the San Francisco General Strike Committee to the Portland workers.

"On Monday morning the general strike was effective beyond all expectations. Nothing moved in or out of the city. For practical utility there are six ways of entrance to the city. These are: (1) Bay Shore Highway; (2) U.S. 101 road; (3) Skyline Boulevard; (4) the ferries; (5) by sea; (6) the railroads. Every one of these ways, excepting the ferries and railroads, was patrolled by our picketing squads of workers. Nothing moved without permission of the strike committee. Within the city, transportation was tied up; production stood at a standstill. It was obvious that the military forces were helpless against such a strike movement.

"In a widely popularized radio address by Governor Merriam that very day, he said: 'By its very nature the general strike challenges the authority and ability of the Government to maintain itself.' " [6]

A similar situation is potentially possible again. The formation of all transport unions into one association such as that being considered at present under the leadership of Hoffa and Bridges carries potentials of great danger. A mass transport strike could so paralyze this country that starvation and death would be rampant in every part. The danger is not limited to America. An international transportation tie up could be fearful in its outreach through all the world.

The mechanism outlined by the Communists is still in operation. It is not completely out of date. Though it has not as yet

---

[6] *The Alliance of Certain Racketeer and Communist Dominated Unions in the Field of Transportation as a Threat to National Security,* Report by the Subcommittee to Investigate the Administration of the Internal Security Act and Other Internal Security Laws to the Committee on the Judiciary, United States Senate, 85th Congress, Second Session, December 17, 1958, United States Government Printing Office, Washington, 1958, pp. 28-30.

fully succeeded in taking over a country, any person of intelligence has great reason for concern when workers can be compelled to join organizations, contribute their money, and obey the leadership imposed by a small group. When that money can be used for political purposes by a constant propaganda campaign by press, radio and television so that the public may be influenced to elect legislators under obligation to the union leadership, the very foundation of republican, democratic government is in danger. When government becomes irreversible, dictatorship is at the door.

VI

SUCCESSFUL TECHNIQUES
FOR SEIZING POWER

THE COMMUNIST attempt to seize power through labor union control has not yet achieved complete victory for the Communists in any country. In those countries where they have established their rule, the means employed have been quite different. The methods by which they achieved power in Russia, China, and Czechoslovakia merit special study. In each case they seized power utilizing deception, established themselves by violence, and maintained their dictatorship by totally enslaving helpless people.

RUSSIA

Revolution broke out in Russia in February, 1917. The Czar was overthrown, and a republican order was established. The declaration of a political amnesty brought into the open the various Russian revolutionary parties. These parties were numerous, and the degree of their revolutionary fervor and devotion to violence varied considerably.

The most moderate of these parties was the Constitutional Democratic Party known as the Cadets. They favored the establishment of a Parliamentary Republic and change via the ballot box.

A second was the historic Russian revolutionary party, the Social Revolutionaries whose program was agrarian reform rather than industrial development. The Social Revolutionaries were also called the populists because of their slogan, "to the people." Desiring to improve the lot of the peasants, young Russian intellectuals went out to the people with their revolutionary message. They advocated land ownership by the peasants themselves. They were not a Marxist Party and did not believe that Russia should follow the pathway of Capitalist development. As their name indicates, they favored radical action and were addicted to violence. Lenin attacked them frequently during his career.

The anarchists were another significant group. They were addicted to violence, assassination and sabotage, and had a long revolutionary tradition and a total contempt for governmental authority of every form.

The Marxists were divided primarily into the Bolsheviks and the Mensheviks, the former being under the leadership of Lenin. As has been related, the Bolsheviks became the Communists.

Finally, there were various independent revolutionary groups, as well as individuals who owed allegiance to no party but were devotees of violent revolutionary action.

These various parties set to work, organized, and published their newspapers. They participated in common organizations known as the soviets. The soviets were born in the 1905 Russian revolution when the historic technique of the mass strike had been tried and had failed. The soviets were committees formed in strategic areas to direct the strike and the revolution. They were called soviets of workers, soldiers and peasants' deputies. Their delegates were elected from the proletariat working in the factories, from the peasantry and from the ranks of the common soldiers and sailors. They began as completely unofficial bodies.

The soviets were re-formed in the days of the Russian Republic after the overthrow of the Czar. The Mensheviks and the Social Revolutionaries were well represented in these soviets. The latter were divided into two groups, Left and Right. The

Bolsheviks were in a small minority in the first half of 1917. The slogan at this time was, "All power to the soviets," but Lenin, filled with a desire to seize complete power in Russia and aware that the soviets were far from being under Bolshevik control, was only half hearted in his support of this slogan.

Meanwhile, Russia was staggering under the blows of the 1914-1918 war. Enormous losses had been suffered on their western front. The soldiers, short of necessary weapons, were in a mutinous mood, while at home, the people were consumed by a desire for peace and for land. Lenin, the dynamic Marxist who seized every opportunity to advance his cause, developed a program which promised peace and land. Everywhere he agitated for the end of the war. He urged the peasants to throw down their arms, return to their homes, and seize the fields of their landlords which, he said, were rightfully theirs. The slogan, "Peace and land," was very popular.

In adopting such a program, Lenin had contravened all the accepted standards of Marxist doctrine. Classical Marxist doctrine had been that private ownership of land was to be replaced by collective ownership. Lenin utterly reversed this policy by promising land to everybody. The other Marxist parties indignantly accused him of stealing the program of the Social Revolutionaries. This is exactly what he had done, brazenly and shamelessly. Lenin was a dynamic Marxist, a believer in the dialectic which, as we will see, allowed him complete freedom of action and policy. If his goal of power could be achieved by doing the exact opposite of what he had long advocated, then that is what he should do. The basic doctrine of Marxism-Leninism is: Come to power. The Marxist-Leninist will promise whatever is necessary in order to achieve that end. Lenin, therefore, promised peace and land. But the gift of land was merely the bait that covered the barbed hook of Communist dictatorship.

It is interesting to notice in passing how Communist policy with regard to the ownership of land varied in the years that followed. In 1917, Lenin gave the land to the peasants, but confiscated the crops when they were harvested. The disgruntled farmers lost their enthusiasm and the harvest diminished. The grain shortage became serious and a desperate famine arose. In 1921, after four years of power, the Communists were on the verge of being overthrown. To avert this, Lenin made a dramatic reversal in policy. He re-established Capitalism. He introduced the New Economic Policy which allowed private trading in grain. Many of the Communists regarded this as a confession of utter defeat and some ideological extremists committed suicide on the streets. But Lenin, regarding the situation in the light of the dialectic, saw it as a temporary withdrawal for future advance.

During the period of the New Economic Policy, the farm produce of Russia increased, and the food situation improved greatly. The Communists, meanwhile, were establishing their power in the cities. By 1928, Stalin, who had succeeded Lenin, felt that they were strong enough to put their real program into operation. He therefore reversed the New Economic Policy, and declared war on the peasants. The most prosperous of the peasants, who were known as "kulaks," were arrested, herded together, and deported to Siberia. The slogan was, "Liquidation of the kulaks as a class." The kulaks were not landlords. The landlords had been annihilated in 1917-18. The kulaks were peasants who had farmed efficiently and employed labor on their farms.

The kulaks' land was made the basis of the collective farms to which the middle and poor peasants were urged to contribute their land and livestock. These peasants, however, resisted attempts to make them join the collectives, preferring to work their own land. When they were forced to join, many of them slaughtered their animals and a great famine rose in the land.

In 1931 Stalin decided to teach the peasants a final lesson. He took all the wheat from the Ukraine and dumped it down in Western Europe, leaving the Ukrainians to starve. During that fearful winter of 1931, it is reported seven million starved to death. Speaking at a meeting in California, I was informed by a young woman who had been a school child in Kiev in the Ukraine at that time that the game they had played on the way to school was counting the dead bodies in the streets. In this manner, Stalin fulfilled Lenin's policy of giving the land to the peasants long enough to consolidate Communist power as a prelude to taking it from them to establish collective ownership which had remained the real objective even while land was being distributed.

However, in mid 1917, all this was in the womb of the future. The war against Germany dragged on, and the situation in Russia became worse. The Bolsheviks gained in popularity through their "peace and land" program, and constantly increased their representation in the soviets by means of their magnificent organization. In July, 1917, they organized a revolt, but it was ill-timed and unsuccessful, and Lenin was forced into hiding. In October of that year, however, the Bolsheviks secured a small majority in the Petrograd Soviet. Lenin decided that the hour of revolution had come, for they could now speak, not only in the name of the Communist Party, but in the name of the soviet which represented the entire working class. The revolution was opposed by some of Lenin's co-workers, particularly Zinoviev and Kamenev, but Lenin's desires dominated, and the revolution was called by the soviet. The Bolshevik-led revolutionaries marched on the Czar's winter palace and arrested the provisional government which was in power until the election of a constituent assembly, and which included many Mensheviks and Social Revolutionaries in its ranks.

The Bolsheviks did not have wide popular support. The only group in the soviet to stand by them at that time was the left wing of the Social Revolutionary Party. Bolshevism thus came to power with a tiny minority of the people, but they established their terror, and Lenin became the ruthless lord and master of Russia.

In all rural areas peasants' committees were formed. These were composed largely of poor peasants and criminal elements. Some were motivated by idealism, while others were motivated by hatred. These aggressive peasant bodies became a key tool of Lenin's reign of terror. He encouraged them to seize the land, kill the landlords and divide the estates among themselves. Frequently the letters ended thus: "Anyone who opposes this is to be shot without mercy."

Resistance to the Communist regime developed in every area of life. The first group to revolt openly were the anarchists who were shot down mercilessly in the streets. Following the anarchists, the Left Wing Social Revolutionaries revolted and met a similar fate.

Confronted with such problems at home, the new regime was faced with the necessity of ending the war against Germany. When the Commander-in-Chief refused to obey the Communist order to lay down arms, Lenin and Stalin telephoned his dismissal and appointed a private as general of the army to conclude the surrender.

Lenin realized that to remain in power he needed a fearful instrument of terror. The Czar had always had a secret police force called the Okrana. The Communists took it over, renamed it the Cheka, and refined and sharpened it into the most fearful instrument of terror the world has ever known. Seeking for a man to head up this organization, Lenin found a remarkable young Polish Bolshevik named Dzerinski. Born of wealthy, aristocratic parents, Dzerinski had, as a child, forsaken the comforts of his home to dedicate himself to the poor of the earth as a revolutionary organizer. His teen-age years were largely spent in Polish prisons where his rule of conduct was that he, as the most enlightened and advanced, was duty bound to perform the most menial tasks. He therefore insisted on cleaning the latrines of the other prisoners as an example of enlightenment and dedication. What better man could Lenin have found to serve as a selfless instrument of murder and extermination? Motivated by his idealistic dedication, Dzerinski became the organizer of the red terror, and the master murderer of modern times.

The story is told that one day as the Bolshevik leaders sat in conference, Lenin asked Dzerinski how many traitorous Social

Revolutionaries they held in prison at that time. Dzerinski replied that there were about fifteen hundred, whereupon Lenin asked for the list so that he might see which were old friends and supporters. Having read the list, Lenin marked the corner of the sheet with a tiny cross. Dzerinski took the sheet, noted the cross, looked at Lenin, and quietly left the room. The following day he informed Lenin that the fifteen hundred had been executed. The cross which Lenin had made to show that he had read the paper had been interpreted as an order for the execution of fifteen hundred people. Lenin had merely intended to indicate that he had read the document. On the misinterpretation of a doodle of Lenin's pencil, fifteen hundred people went to their death.

Communist power in Russia was consolidated by limitless, pitiless violence. Lenin had said, "What does it matter if three quarters of the world perish provided the remaining quarter is Communist!" Any act of terror was justified if it assured continuing Communist control. Group by group, the opposing forces were liquidated until at last the impossible was achieved and the Communist Party held Russia in total enslavement. When the Communist monster had devoured all other revolutionary groups, it turned and destroyed most of its own creators.

CHINA

The Communist conquest of China is a classical manifestation of the five steps of Communist conquest:

1. The conquest of the student mind
2. The organization of the students into the Communist Party
3. The scientific exploitation of group self interest to bring that party to popularity and power
4. Revolutionary conquest of power
5. Communist dictatorship and universal slavery.

1. The Conquest of the Student Mind

The students in China were a very special class. The scholar was always an object of veneration to the Chinese and the influence of the students was very considerable. The Communists were highly successful in recruiting students into the ranks of the Communist Party. Almost the entire leadership of the Chinese Communist Party joined that Party as students. The arguments used to recruit the student intellectual have already been discussed.

2. Organization of Students into the Communist Party

The Communist Party of China was formed on typical Leninist lines. The inner core came from the ranks of the intellectuals. The bulk of the general membership came from the peasants. The members derived from the working class were few indeed. This is a peculiar structure for a party claiming to be proletarian. The Party was formed with a single leader, Mao Tse-tung. With complete discipline the entire Party membership absorbed the thought and obeyed the orders of Mao Tse-tung.

3. Scientific Exploitation of Group Self-Interest

The disciplined, fanatical Communist cadres worked feverishly among the masses of the people. Their objective was not to convert them to the theories of Communism, but to exploit their desires and grievances. Many of the Chinese people were landless tenant farmers. A great burden of debt hung round their shoulders. Their burning desires were centered round the ownership of the land on which they labored, and freedom from their burden of debt.

The Communist approach was therefore very simple. They promised the people the ownership of the land on which they worked and the abolition of all debt. In addition, China had known the oppression of foreign power, so the Communists exploited Chinese nationalism with a program to exclude the white man from Asia. With such a program so closely tuned to the deep-seated desires of the masses of the people, it is easy to understand why the Communists achieved a certain popularity. From the peasants attracted by the Communist promises, Mao Tse-tung gathered the youth, trained them with great efficiency, and built the Chinese Communist Army.

4. Revolutionary Conquest of Power

The conquest of China was successfully accomplished through the strategy of the brilliant Chinese Communist leader, Mao Tse-tung. He developed two new techniques which were in large measure responsible for Communist success in the face of great odds. The first of these was the principle of political warfare in association with military conflict. The war was waged not only by the armed forces, but by political agents as well who always preceded the Communist soldiers into any given area. Their task was to infiltrate and to undermine the will of the people to resist. They spread rumor and utilized blackmail and terror. They took advantage of civil liberty to destroy civil liberty. They combined assassination with sabotage so effectively that many communities were neutralized and fell easy prey to the Communist military advance. No advance was made by Communist troops until the way had been prepared by the Communist political agents.

The second technique developed by Mao Tse-tung was that of guerilla warfare. By means of this art, he was able to transform strategic inferiority into tactical superiority. Although his army was outnumbered for many years, he was able to manipulate his troops with such skill that he never engaged in pitched battle unless he outnumbered the enemy by three to one. He was able to achieve this because of the superior mobility of his troops and by the technique of guerilla warfare which he perfected. He would gather together a considerable number of his soldiers in a given area, launch a lightning offensive against the enemy at a point where they were gathered in smaller number, and disappear with his troops before the enemy could rally. His soldiers would hide their uniforms, adopt the character of the surrounding peasantry, and mingle with the people. By the time the superior forces of the enemy had gathered, the Communist army was nowhere to be found. By this dual offensive of political warfare and guerilla mobility, the Chinese Communist forces advanced to victory, conquering the vast land mass of China.

In addition to the internal forces operating within China, the International Communist machine worked ceaselessly on their behalf. Russia provided military instructors and weapons. Throughout the world the Chinese Communists were pictured as benign agrarian reformers and the Chiang Kai-Shek government as the epitome of corruption. The American government endeavored to achieve the impossible, establish a permanent, peaceful co-existence between Communism and the Chinese government. This played right into Communist hands and after the defeat of Japan, Russia delivered the vast weapon hoard of the Japanese Manchurian Army to the Chinese Communists, and their successful southward march began.

5. Communist Dictatorship and Universal Slavery

Once in power the Communist Party systematically set about the process of securing a monopoly over the lives of all Chinese citizens so that the Party could remain all-powerful permanently while the people were reduced to the impotence of isolated slaves. Every vestige of alternative authority was smashed. The Communist Party secured a monopoly of all police power, all economic power, all military and educational power. It became the universal policeman, employer, administrator, judge, newsman, entertainer and teacher. It imposed the "Dictatorship of the Proletariat."

CZECHOSLOVAKIA

The means adopted by the Communists for the conquest of Czechoslovakia differ somewhat from those used in Russia and China. Since it is closer to the method which they probably envisage for the conquest of America, it merits some attention. They came to power in Czechoslovakia by utilizing an internal Communist minority which operated in the blackmailing shadow of massive external Russian military power. Hanging like a threatening cloud over Czechoslovakia was the Red Army.

At the conclusion of the second World War, Czechoslovakia was the most industrialized, the most prosperous, and the most democratic of the Eastern European states. Communism was an insignificant force. Three years later Czechoslovakia was bound hand and foot as a Communist slave. This was brought to pass by a series of small concessions to Communism, each relatively insignificant in itself, each presented as an alternative to attack by the Red Army, and obviously to be preferred to such an attack. The cumulative effect, however, was the surrender of Czechoslovakia to Communism. This is the program for America. The concessions are to be obtained because they are preferable to an atomic war. Each in itself may appear indecisive, but each will be a step to surrender. Every time the Communists can persuade Americans the false alternative exists, that is, to make this concession as the only alternative to atomic or thermonuclear war, they win a great victory.

Within Czechoslovakia, government was administered by various departments of executive authority, each department being headed by a cabinet minister. Authority in each department of government was thus largely centralized in the hands of one man. Police power, for example, was in the hands of the Minister of Internal Security. This applied in education, communications, transportation, agriculture, justice and defense.

The first step taken by the Communist minority was to estab

lish themselves in a coalition government with democratic and socialist parties. They then proceeded to infiltrate Communists into the top positions in all branches of government. Once the top position in each department of government was filled by a Communist, non-Communists and anti-Communists within the organization were powerless to withstand his total authority and power. When, for example, the Communists took over the police force, they used the power so gained to arrest and destroy all those who differed from them politically, including those to whom they had temporarily showed friendship. Thus did Communism take over the most democratic nation in Eastern Europe. It is to be noted that it was not done by the use of the Red Army, but simply by the threat of its use.

It is a program of this nature which the Communists probably envisage for America. When America is encircled economically, and militarily, when foreign markets are disrupted and foreign trade destroyed, when America is an island in a Communist sea, and lies under the shadow of military annihilation, the Communists believe that America will make concessions as did Czechoslovakia. Authority will be centralized and a few Communists will wield great power. At the chosen moment the final Communist assault will take place and resistance will be token and half-hearted.

VII

CONSOLIDATION OF POWER—
The Dictatorship of the Proletariat

WHEN ONCE the Communists have come to power, whether it be in Russia, China, Czechoslovakia, or America, the next step is to establish the dictatorship of the proletariat. Lenin defined this as "the rule—unrestricted by law and based on force—of the proletariat over the bourgeoisie, a rule enjoying the sympathy and support of the laboring and exploited masses." [1] This rule is theoretically exercised by the proletariat, or, in other words, by the toiling masses of the people. But since the Communist Party considers itself the executive of the proletariat, this rule is exercised in practice by the Communist Party. The definition of the dictatorship of the proletariat, then, is "the rule, based on force and unrestricted by law, of the Communist Party over everybody else."

Since this rule is based on force, the first act of Communist power is invariably to disarm the people as was done in China. Since this rule is based on force, and since force inevitably generates revolt, a second precaution taken by the Communists is to destroy the potential leadership of a counter revolution before such a revolution can occur. Any individual with qualities of leadership who is not subject to Communist discipline is arrested

[1] Quoted by Joseph Stalin, *Problems of Leninism* (Moscow: Foreign Languages Publishing House, 1953), p. 51.

and executed. Whether he is pro-Communist or anti-Communist is immaterial. If he has qualities of leadership which may be used when the people awaken and desire to end Communist rule, he is a danger and must be destroyed.

The dictatorship of the proletariat is accompanied by a monopoly of the means of communication by the Communist Party. Every medium of mass communication is taken over. Every newspaper is a Communist newspaper. Every radio station, every television channel, every publishing house, every book, every magazine, every school class is completely controlled by the Communist Party.

Under the dictatorship of the proletariat, an economic monopoly is gradually established whereby the Communist Party becomes the sole employer. A man then has but one choice—he works for the Communist Party where he is told to work, or he starves to death. He may not leave his job and go to another, for there is only one employer—the Communist Party.

Yet another feature of the dictatorship of the proletariat is the establishment of a vast, internal espionage network. This espionage system is patterned on the human body. The body is made up of billions of cells. The body preserves itself against the external forces which threaten it by a vast grouping of espionage agents. Certain cells become informers. Physiologically, they are called sensory receptors and are to be found in the skin, muscles and various organs. These sensory receptors perceive heat, cold, pain, and contact with other objects. In other words, they collect information from their environment and send it to the brain. The brain assembles this information and sends orders down another nerve pathway to the executive authority, the muscles, whereupon muscular reaction is taken in relation to the information collected by those sensory nerve cells in the environment. The simple act of blinking which closes the eyelids to protect the sensitive eye against an advancing foreign body is a good example of such a mechanism.

The Communists see the State, not as a mass of individuals,

but as an organic unity, a higher form of being. Just as the body has sensory receptors, so throughout the State there are informers who collect information in their environment and send it back to the central nervous system—the secret police. Children are set to spy on their parents, wives on their husbands, employees on employers, pastors on their congregations, parishioners on their pastors. Every group, large or small, would have in its midst a number of informers. None of these informers would know who the others were. If one informed and the others did not, those failing to report would automatically be discovered. Thus a stream of information from every segment of the community flows back to the central authority.

With such a system in existence, it is inevitable that a revolt that has any organization whatsoever will be discovered at birth and strangled in infancy.

In the days of the Czar, a thousand men armed with sticks and stones were quite a formidable force. If revolution broke out somewhere in Siberia, it took three months for the news to reach Moscow and six months for troops to get there and quell the uprising. With modern means of communication, however, the news is back in seconds, and an air force detachment is there in minutes to deal with the trouble. The people are helpless against machine guns and bombs. The question is frequently asked: "Is it likely that the people of Russia will revolt?" Of course they will. They have already revolted a thousand times! But the revolts are spasmodic and unorganized, and they are wiped out almost casually. Ten miles away it is not even known that the revolt has taken place because of the power of the Communist dictatorship.

The steps by which the dictatorship of the proletariat was established in China show the situation very clearly. The Communists came to power in China behind the seductive promises of land ownership and debt abolition. Immediately after seizing power, they kept these promises. The landlords were wiped out and their land was divided and given to the peasants whose debts were simultaneously cancelled. For a brief period happiness flooded the land. The peasants set to work to till the land which was now theirs.

Meanwhile, the Communists consolidated their power in anticipation of the day when they could take away the land from the peasants. They knew that when they did this, resistance would develop, and that such resistance would require leadership. They surveyed the community to discover those with potentials of leadership. If these people were not subject to Communist discipline, they were arrested on some pretext or another and destroyed.

The Communists set about to disarm the people completely. Great rewards were given to those who could tell where weapons were hidden, and the rush to deliver concealed weapons began. They introduced a system of universal espionage in which everyone spied on everyone else. This had special reference to the children who were encouraged to spy and report on their own parents.

They stopped freedom of movement and introduced internal passports. No one could travel from village to village without official permission. Upon arriving at the village, the visitor was not free to go and stay with friends, but had to stay at an inn set aside by the Communists and closely scrutinized by them. They stopped freedom of association. No group could gather except under official Communist sponsorship and control.

Every individual was compelled to write or give a life confession detailing all the crimes committed throughout his entire life and naming all other persons implicated in these crimes. This provided the Communist government with a vast hoard of information to be used against any individual as they desired.

A major assault was made on the child mind. They were filled with pride. Their affections were turned from their parents towards the State. They were given guns and appointed sentries with orders to challenge and, if necessary, to shoot adults. The school children would be marched out and given the task of searching all shops in an area for weapons and currency, and of accosting and searching all adults in the area.

Finally there came the day of the mass trials and executions. A band would march through the streets of the city. Behind the band a group of prisoners would march with hands bound behind their backs. Into the bonds of each prisoner a stick would be stuck with a placard on top telling the crimes of which he was allegedly guilty. Behind the prisoners the school children would march to observe the execution. Then came the general populace. Mothers were compelled to take their babies in arms to observe the hideous spectacle. Eye witness reports abound concerning these things. Multitudes of missionaries of impeccable character testify that these things really happened.

Harvest day arrived and the peasants who had been so thrilled to become owners of their land were now forbidden to thresh their own grain except in the presence of an armed soldier. When the harvest was reaped, the government took far more than the landlords had ever taken.

At this point hatred of Communism was the dominant emotion amongst the people, but they were so leaderless, so weaponless, so immobilized, so disassociated, so spied upon and so cowed that organized revolt appeared unattainable. The Communists had imposed their total tyranny.

The period of peasant land ownership was brief indeed. Soon came the period of collective farms and then the great communes which have attacked the very fabric of the Chinese nation, the Chinese family and the character of the Chinese people. No Chinese individual now owns one acre of ground. He has been betrayed to a new serfdom more terrible than that of the past, a serfdom in which he is the helpless slave of the gargantuan Communist State.

The dictatorship becomes ever more intense. The powers in the hands of the top few become greater and greater until finally there emerges the man of all power, the Joseph Stalin, who sits in the seat of the mighty while millions of slaves rush to and fro to do his bidding. Such is the reign of brutality, violence and tyranny which inevitably comes behind the beautiful promise with which Communism deceives its way to power. Only knowledge can enable us to stand against the intermediate seductive phase of limitless deception practised by those whom J. Edgar Hoover defines as "Masters of Deceit."

VIII

ALLIES OF COMMUNISM

THE SIGNIFICANCE of Communism can never be measured by the number of Communists. Lenin's slogan was "fewer but better." It has been a long-established slogan that "the Party grows strong through purging itself." The theory of Communism is that of the chosen few who are organized, disciplined, dedicated, and equipped with superior intelligence and understanding of the laws of history. By this chosen few, the conquest of the world and the regeneration of mankind will be accomplished. The number of actual Communists has never been great.

Even acute observers, noting the numerical weakness of the Communists, have taken false hope from this fact. Such people fail to understand that the Communists are able to rally into their service multitudes who are completely unaware that they are serving the Communist cause. Our purpose here is to study those attitudes which transform well-meaning, patriotic, Christian people into the allies of Communism.

INTELLECTUAL DISHONESTY

Outstanding among these attitudes is intellectual dishonesty. When the truth is too unpleasant, a natural tendency is to refuse to believe it. As a medical man, I have seen this often. A man of character and intelligence is afflicted with cancer. He knows the symptoms perfectly well, and if he saw them in another, would never have a moment's doubt about the final outcome. When he observes these symptoms in himself, however, a strange thing happens. His characteristic honesty and clarity of judgment disappear. He ignores the central, symptomatic stream, and seizing on peripheral symptoms, builds them into a dream world in which to take refuge while doom advances.

No matter how clear the evidence is, people can always find an interpretation that will allow them to cling to what they want to believe. This is well illustrated by the story of the priest and the rabbi who were driving along the road, the rabbi in front and the priest behind. As they approached the intersection, the rabbi gently stood on the brakes and brought his car to a halt. The priest, however, had been gazing all round the countryside. Noticing at last that he was right on top of the rabbi's car, he jammed on the brakes, but to no avail. He crashed into the rear of the rabbi's car.

The priest and the rabbi were surveying the damage when along came an Irish policeman. After he had examined the wreck and had ascertained the respective owners of the two cars, he was clearly a man in great mental and emotional distress. He found himself in the grip of two simultaneous, conflicting duties, his duty to the Church and his duty to the law. He began to tremble and stammer. Suddenly the answer to his prayer came. The wrinkles left his brow, and a look of confidence and serenity came over his face. He looked sternly at the rabbi, and then, turning to the priest, he asked, "Father, what speed was this man doing when he backed into you?" How often the wish begets the thought.

The situation confronting us is dark and fearful. To face the true situation requires courage and honesty. The vast majority of people are quite unwilling to acknowledge the truth, preferring to ignore the evidence, or to select only those facts which will support their preconceived ideas and will not threaten the fulfilment of their desires.

Some time ago I met a man I had long admired. As a journalist sympathetic to the Soviet government, he had been sent to Russia in the 1930's. There he discovered what was really taking place, and set out to inform the world of the truth about Communism. He wrote splendid books which influenced me profoundly when I read them some years ago. When I met him, I thanked him for what he had done, and told him how greatly his books had influenced me. He looked at me with a gloomy expression and said, "It didn't do much good, did it? When I wrote those books, the Communists had a hundred and sixty million. Now they have a billion. Western civilization is doomed. We are as certain to become extinct as the Indian civilization was before the advance of the white man."

You may dismiss this man as an abject pessimist if you will, but you cannot so easily dispose of the facts. If we weigh the evidence of impending Communist conquest by any of the standard methods of judging human knowledge, it is very difficult to escape the conclusion which he reached. This evidence may be considered under five headings:

1. The numerical evidence
2. The military evidence
3. The economic evidence
4. The educational evidence
5. The communications evidence.

1. *The Numerical Evidence*

In the year 1903, Lenin established the movement called Bolshevism with seventeen supporters. In the year 1917, Lenin conquered Russia with a Party of approximately forty thousand members. By 1959, the party of Lenin had conquered one billion people. In one generation, the godless Communists have brought under their control twelve times as many as Hitler ruled at the beginning of World War II, twelve times as many as Japan ruled, and six times the population of the United States. In less than half a century, they have conquered far more than the total number of the world's population who have heard the minimum story of Christ from any source after nearly two thousand years. Those who have heard of Christ from any source—Protestant, Catholic, Jehovah's Witness, Mormon, or Christian Scientist—add up to approximately seven hundred and fifty million. In one generation the Communists have conquered a billion. There are in the world today five children in school learning in detail the godless doctrines of Communism, for every one child in any school anywhere learning anything about Christ. These facts are fearful to contemplate, but they are inescapably true.

These figures are the more frightening when they are examined as any honest businessman would examine them. I spoke in St. Louis, Missouri, to the management club of a small but very prosperous firm. The president of the firm told me that he wanted to show me the secret of their success. Taking me into a room, he showed me an electronic computer. Said he, "We are not satisfied to know the past and the present. We need to know the future. At last we have found how to discover the future. This machine is the answer. We feed into it the figures of the past and we get from it the predictions of the future. Those predictions are so accurate, that upon them we base our production and marketing schedules." The machine was so valuable that they were paying over $2,000 a month rental for it though they were a small company employing only about three hundred people.

I said to him, "Here is a set of figures to feed into the machine. Lenin established Bolshevism with seventeen supporters in 1903. He conquered Russia with forty thousand in 1917. Today, the party of Lenin has conquered one billion. The population of the world is two and three quarter billion. By what year will that figure be reached?"

He replied, "I'm frightened to try it."

He had every reason to be frightened. The result would have been terrifying indeed.

2. *The Military Evidence*

The oceans that surround America, traditionally the barrier of protection against the enemy, have become the source of an infinite danger. The Communists have at their disposal some five hundred submarines. Many of these are long range, and many can fire missiles which have a radius of several hundred miles. They can carry an atomic or thermo-nuclear warhead. At any time the Communist leader so chooses, submarines can emerge from the waters of the Pacific, the Atlantic, and the Gulf of Mexico, discharge their guided missiles, and submerge. Simultaneously, Washington, D.C., Baltimore, Philadelphia, Boston, Miami, New Orleans, Houston, San Diego, Los Angeles, San Francisco, Portland, and Seattle could be wiped from the face of the earth. The power to do this is in being right now. There is no effective defense against it. It is true that the United States could retaliate through her Strategic Air Command, and by means of her missiles located in Europe. Should she do so, devastation in Russia would be terrible indeed. But this would not bring back to life one destroyed American citizen, or rebuild from the vapors one shattered city.

Richard Arens, director of the House Un-American Activities Committee, tells how they called before their committee the military man they considered best equipped to deal with the subject of Communism, General Wedemeyer, aide to General MacArthur in the Far East. Arens asked him, "General Wedemeyer, how late do you consider it to be on the Communist timetable for world conquest?"

General Wedemeyer thought for a few moments, and then replied, "Too late. If I were advising the Communist leaders, I would say, 'Don't change one thing you are doing. You are winning as certainly as any group ever won any battle in the history of mankind.'"

At the conclusion of the general's testimony, Richard Arens

asked, "General, in the light of these frightening things that you have told us, what do you advise that we should do?"

General Wedemeyer replied, "Had you asked me that question fifteen years ago, I could have answered it with ease. Had you asked it ten years ago, I could have answered it with difficulty. When you ask it today, the only honest reply that I can make is that I do not know."

Big business in America takes considerable trouble to make long range future predictions. In one city they have established what is known as a "think center." Here they have gathered together the finest electronic equipment and skilled personnel to make these predictions. Into the equipment they fed all the data they were able to collect related to the relative war-making capacities of America and Russia to determine by what year the balance of power would be favorable to Russia in a future war. The date delivered by the machine was the year 1965.

3. *The Educational Evidence*

By a tremendous concentration on education, the Communists are today graduating in Russia alone three times as many engineers and scientists as the United States. When their China program matures, they will graduate ten times as many. They are graduating, at a rough estimate, one hundred times as many language specialists. When their China program matures, their linguistic superiority will be astronomical.

A common reaction to this information is to draw comfort from the fact that in Communist countries there is no academic freedom. One of the great delusions of American educators has been that academic freedom is necessary for the achievement of material results. If a child is trained in habits of study, and then forced to study mathematics, science, and foreign languages, he will learn a lot whether the system is free or not. Regimentation and tyranny have always been able to achieve great things. The pharaohs built the pyramids; the Chinese built the Great

Wall of China; Hitler achieved miracles in Germany, and there is no evidence whatsoever that he had any trouble controlling his educated classes. Under an authoritarian system of regimented education, the Germans made tremendous progress in the science of rocketry and electronics, and in the development of the jet aircraft. In a similar way, the Communists with their emphasis on science, foreign languages, and mathematics, are making tremendous progress. It is not a question of which system of education develops better balanced personalities. The question is: Which system of education will win this universal war?

I was visiting an American college. Before I had been there ten minutes, the president told me with great pride of a young man who had brought glory and honor to their school. Wherever I went on that campus, I heard his praises sung. At last I met him, and a fine young man he was. His body was lithe and slender, and he stood some six feet two inches tall. He was their leading basketball player. His skill at the game was so great that he had been chosen to go to Melbourne, Australia, to represent the United States in the Olympic Games in 1956. What an honor for the school!

But when I asked, "Who is your leading science student?" he looked at me in wonder and amazement. He could not answer the question. To find out information like that a careful study of the records would be required.

I want to make it quite clear that I have nothing against basketball. I think it is a splendid sport. The ability to project accurately an inflated spherical ball through an iron hoop is a remarkable gift indeed. However, it is difficult to envisage how ballistic missiles can be effectively stopped with basketballs. Faced as we are with a struggle for survival against an enemy who spares no effort to educate the young in those fields which will help to secure victory, it would seem that the scale of values in the American educational system might well be revised.

4. *The Economic Evidence*

If we were to plot on a graph the total economic product of
Russia and America and their rates of growth, the lines would
cross within a measurable period ahead. The exact length of that
period of time has been variously estimated. A few years ago it
was said that they would cross within fifteen years. Khrushchev
has claimed that they will overtake America within seven years.
All authorities agree that the gap between Russian and American
production is closing.

The problem, however, is not merely that the Russian total
economic product may soon equal that of America. The great
problem lies in the percentage of the Russian economic product
that is available to the Communists for class warfare. Because
the Communist Party has a monopoly ownership of the entire
Russian economic product, it can use the economic product as it
will. Because of their monopoly ownership, the Communists can
decide how much the individual Russian may have, and how
much of the total product will be retained to be used in economic
warfare against the United States. By keeping the people at a
very low standard of living, they are able to use a large propor-
tion of their economic product to destroy American foreign markets by underselling the American product.

Monopoly has a tremendous advantage in competition with
small industry. Unprotected by law, no small concern with only
a few employees could stand against any of the great national
corporations. Were it not for the protection afforded by anti-
trust laws, a big chain store could very easily put out of operation
the little grocer on the corner. All the chain store would need
to do would be to open up a market nearby. Since this market
would be only one of hundreds owned by them, they would not
need to make a profit. They could undersell on every line. Their
little competitor, however, has limited financial resources. He
has to make a profit to pay his debts and to carry on his business.

The time he can compete is limited. In time his resources are exhausted and he is forced to close down.

The Communists are doing a similar thing on a world scale. They can move into any American foreign market they consider desirable. They do not need to make a profit; their profit is in the chaos they create in the American economy, in the agents they infiltrate into the country through their trade.

An example of Communist techniques of economic warfare may be seen in their activities in Iraq. Iraq had vast sums secured from oil royalties to be invested in developmental projects. A large number of the contracts for these projects went to Russia. To secure a contract, the Communists followed this simple procedure: they found out from pro-Communist elements in the Iraqi government the lowest bid made by any Western firm, and tendered a bid twenty per cent below it. They did not need to make a profit directly for their profit was in the Communist agents they infiltrated and the subversive literature they distributed, as well as in the weakening of the American economy. It is difficult to see how any concern that must make a profit to survive can compete against them.

The advancing Communist economic penetration is causing grave concern among business leaders and the governmental authorities. The situation grows more serious year by year.

5. *The Evidence in the Field of Communications*

The world is divided into three major areas: there is the Communist area, a great prison containing a billion slaves; there is what is known as the Free World consisting of America and her allies; and between these two, there is the vast, uncommitted area of the world which numbers one billion people. This uncommitted area is composed primarily of the new nations of Asia and Africa. With them should be included the nations of Central and South America. These countries are the great battle ground between East and West. If the Communists secure them, they will have two billion and their superiority will be absolute. If the

Free World can keep them outside the Communist fold, there may be some hope of maintaining the present unstable balance of power.

The peoples of these countries are being wooed and won by the Communists, not with bombs and bullets, but with words and books. One hundred people are being reached with Communist lies for every one being reached with the Christian or the democratic truth. The Communists are engaged in the greatest literature crusade mankind has ever known. They are producing beautiful literature in almost every language and distributing it in every corner of the earth. In many countries this literature costs practically nothing. An example of this is *Problems of Leninism* by Joseph Stalin. This book of more than eight hundred pages may be purchased in a Communist bookstore in America for four dollars; in Canada it costs a dollar and fifty cents; in Australia, it costs seventy cents; in India or Japan it may be purchased for ten cents. The price charged has no relationship to the cost of production; it is related merely to the economic capacity of the purchasers.

An example of their beautiful color magazines is *China Pictorial* which is printed in Peking every two weeks in Chinese, Mongolian, Tibetan, Uighur, Korean, English, Russian, German, French, Japanese, Viet-namese, Indonesian, Hindi, Spanish, Arabic and Burmese. Every face wears a radiant smile. The color photography is beautiful. The moral tone is excellent: there is no violence, no crime, no nakedness, no sex, and no alcohol. Every page portrays abundance, beauty, prosperity, liberty and peace. You cannot look through such a magazine without being impressed.

How thoroughly the Communists are carrying out this literary crusade is indicated by the children's books which they are producing in practically every language. Visit any Communist bookstore in the United States and you will find books printed in Moscow and Peking in English for one, two and three-year-old babies. These have titles such as *The Rose and the Earthworm, The Golden Ass, The Little Bird Who Hurt His Wing, The Cater-*

pillar, Punchy the Elephant, Chickens and Ears, The Lamb and the Wolf, The Ant and the Grasshopper, The Adventures of the Little Swallow, How the Monkeys Reached for the Moon, Beautiful Leaves, Wow-wow's House, Tolstoy's Short Stories. The Communists want the children. They do not care so much about the adults whom they consider as already contaminated with the disease of Capitalism and consequently of little use to them. When the Communists rule the world, the diseased social classes will have to be eliminated. But the children are different. They can do something with them. This children's literature is a preliminary step towards winning the children of the world.

An examination of some of the children's literature produced by the Communists induces bewilderment in most loyal Americans, for they can discover nothing wrong with these books. The stories are well told, beautifully illustrated, and do not teach Communism in any way. The trouble with these books is that there is nothing wrong with them.

If a kidnapper wishes to gain the confidence of a child to entice her into an automobile for dreadful purposes, he does not give a long lecture about what will happen after she gets into the automobile. He gives her candy to win her confidence. The candy he gives is not bitter or poisoned candy, for the sweeter and better the candy, the greater the likelihood that the child will get into the automobile. These children's books are the Communist literary candy with which the Communists are endeavoring to entice the children of the world into the Communist automobile for their journey into slavery and death.

The Communists divide their literature into two categories: Propaganda and Agitation. Propaganda they define as that which conveys many ideas to a few people. Propaganda teaches Communist theory, philosophy, organization and doctrine. It is designed primarily for the thinking, student mind.

For the many, they publish Agitation. Agitation they define as that which conveys one idea to many people. The Communists' great literary crusade is designed to convey to the people of the world the simple idea that wherever Communism comes to power, the people immediately become happy, healthy, prosperous and free, whereas America is evil and degenerate, and a threat to the peace of the entire world. The Communists are reaching one hundred people with these blatant lies for every one being reached with the Christian or democratic truth.

The truth is very simple. No matter what promises Communism makes, this fact stands out with crystal clarity: wherever people can escape from Communist rule, they do it by the million. Try to imagine what it would take to cause parents to gather together their children and what few articles they could carry in their arms, and go on foot into the night, not to a bright future, but to the bleak unknown. How bad would things have to be to cause people to do that? Millions are doing this wherever Communism comes to power. When faced with these unanswerable facts, the Communist spokesmen are helpless.

During his visit to the United States, Nikita Khrushchev was asked the following question by Karl Feller, president of the International Union of United Brewery, Flour, Cereal, Soft Drink and Distillery Workers of America: "Mr. Chairman, I cannot understand, since the Communist Party proclaims itself to be the liberator of the working class, yet we see a mass exodus of workers in other countries following the Communist seizure of power. You have the example of three million workers fleeing from East Germany to West Berlin, and about three million fleeing from North Korea to South Korea and, as mentioned a moment ago, three hundred or so thousands of Hungarians braved arrest and death in escaping to freedom. Mr. Khrushchev, can you tell us of a single instance where, following Communist seizure of power, there has been a mass influx of workers from surrounding non-Communist countries into the Communist country? If the Communist Party is the liberator of the working class, why don't we see this phenomenon?"

Mr. Khrushchev: "Is that all? Think it over. Drink your beer. Perhaps that will help you to find the answer to your question."

Mr. Feller: "That certainly is no answer, and apparently nothing will make you understand why millions want to escape from Communism—"

Mr. Khrushchev: "I've told you, I'm not even afraid of the devil." [1]

There are many things which may be said by way of criticism of America, but when all has been said, the fact remains that America is the magnet that draws to its shores people from all over the world. It is still the land of hope and promise, a vision living in the hearts and minds of millions. The unfortunate thing is that these facts do not speak for themselves. They must be made known by the means of communication. By an extensive and effective use of the means of communication, the Communists have convinced two thirds of the people of the world that the exact opposite of these facts is true. A lie that is believed has great power for evil.

An honest consideration of the evidence—numerical, military, economic, educational, and communicational—is frightening indeed. The most comforting thing to do is to put it out of the mind or to refuse to believe it. This is the attitude adopted by a large number of people.

While visiting Philadelphia, I went to a radio station at eleven o'clock one night to be interviewed. A psychiatrist was to be interviewed at the same radio station on the subject of mental health. His interview was to follow mine. He arrived early, and we talked for some minutes before I went on the air. During that time, I gathered that he was quite unsympathetic towards my position and viewpiont.

When I went on the air, I explained, as I frequently do, that my greatest problem is to persuade people that Communists are Communists. Just as the Catholics are Catholics and have certain beliefs and programs, the Communists are Communists and have clear beliefs, and a very well developed program. The aim

---

[1] *U.S. News and World Report,* October 5, 1959, p. 95. Excerpts from a discussion between Nikita Khrushchev and American labor leaders at a meeting in San Francisco, September 21, 1959.

of their program is to conquer the world. The realization of the plan necessitates the encirclement and demoralization of the United States, leading finally to surrender. I pointed out that many intelligent people are unwilling to acknowledge that these things are so, even though all the facts point in this direction.

I went on to describe how the program of the Communists is being fulfilled. While America is being lulled to sleep with a false picture of friendship and talk about co-existence, the Communists are making devastating progress in many parts of the world. They are operating in all the Asian countries, in Africa and the Near East, and are looking forward to the time when Western Europe will be economically strangulated and defenseless; they are invading South and Central America by their infiltration of the colleges and universities. When these countries have been taken, America, isolated, confused, and demoralized, economically and militarily encircled, will be offered the choice of surrender or annihilation. The Communists are certain that she will choose surrender.

As I was speaking, the psychiatrist seethed. At last he could stand no more and spontaneously came onto the program to try and counteract the damage I was doing. When a man's evidence cannot be discredited, the simplest alternative is to discredit the man himself. This he proceeded to do. He told the listening audience that I was apparently the victim of certain deep-seated, inner, emotional conflicts which I was projecting into my external environment. Out of this inner conflict sprang this vision of a great encircling force. The inference was clearly my need of psychiatric treatment.

When he had finished speaking, I thanked him very much for giving me the perfect example of what I had been talking about. Here was an apparently intelligent man who was quite unwilling to face the truth. I had with me the book *How to be a Good Communist*. I showed him that the author was Liu Shao-chi, President of Communist China. I opened the book and asked him to read: "What is the most fundamental and common duty of us Communist Party members? As everybody knows, it is to establish Communism, to transform the present world into a Communist world." [2]   On another page I showed him the following passage:

> . . . the cause of Communism has become a powerful, invincible force throughout the world. There is not the slightest doubt that this force will continue to develop and advance and will win final and complete victory. Despite this, however, the strength of the international reactionary forces and of the exploiting classes are still more powerful than ours, and for the time being are still predominant in many respects. Consequently, we shall have to go through a long, bitter, circuitous and arduous process of struggle before we defeat them.[3]

When he had finished reading, the psychiatrist indicated that I was putting my own interpretation on these passages and giving my own opinion as fact.

"In the name of all that's honest," I replied, "please tell me what other interpretation these words can have, 'the fundamental duty of Communist Party members is to transform the present world into a Communist world'?"

We have always had people in our midst who thought that fire would not burn, that if you jump out of a tenth story window, you may go down, but then again, you may go up. We used to call it insanity. Only recently has it taken to itself the name of mental health.

The malady of intellectual dishonesty has afflicted large segments of the educated and the religious groups leaving them quite unable to face the unpleasant truth. Intellectual dishonesty is one of the greatest allies of Communism. Like cancer, it cannot be treated adequately till its malignancy is recognized.

CULTURAL INTERCHANGE

A second ally of Communism is the naive belief that the truth about Communism can be learned by superficial observation. An idea which has currently gained wide acceptance is that legiti-

---

[2] Liu Shao-chi, *op. cit.*, p. 37.
[3] *Ibid.*, p. 41.

mate information about Communism may be secured by a brief visit to a Communist country.

As I travel throughout America lecturing on Communism, I am frequently asked if I have visited Russia. The inference is that if I have not, I cannot possibly understand very much about Communism. To audiences which pose this question, I reply that I have not been to Russia and that I realize that this is a serious disadvantage. I then express the hope that after I have outlined my qualifications, they will all feel moved to contribute generously in order to send me. To prove my qualifications for such a visit I proceed to give them the fruit of my acute observations concerning America. I have been in America, on and off, for about nine years. I have travelled in forty-six states; I have addressed hundreds of thousands of people, and have enjoyed complete freedom of movement and freedom of speech. As far as I know, I have never been followed by an agent of any investigative group, or by the police. As an Australian, I speak the English language exceedingly well, though I have great difficulty persuading Americans that this is so. During this time, therefore, I have had ample opportunity to observe America and Americans.

The first thing that astonished me when I arrived was that apparently nobody approved of the character or record of President Roosevelt. In Australia we had thought him to be a universal American hero. When the first fifty people to whom I spoke unanimously castigated him, I received the shock of my life. During my nine years in this country, I have never heard a Negro complain of discrimination though I have addressed thousands and conversed with hundreds of them. I have never seen a violent crime; I have never witnessed a major automobile accident; I have never seen a basketball match; and, as far as I know, I have never seen a professional gambler or a prostitute. After ten years of personal, first hand observation, I make my report: "Inside America" by Fred C. Schwarz. "Nobody in America voted for President Roosevelt; no Negro is concerned with discrimination; there is no violent crime; there are no automobile accidents; nobody plays basketball; there is no gambling and there is no prostitution." This is the truth because I have been there and I have seen it for myself.

If someone would just send me to Russia for three weeks or so, I could bring back the truth about what is happening over there. Admittedly I would be slightly handicapped because I cannot speak the language. However, this is not really important because the Communist government thought of it long in advance and has made adquate provision for it. They have trained as interpreters some of their finest young Communists who are totally dedicated to the Party, and very quick of mind and tongue. These interpreters have a three-fold task. In the first place, they are to take me round and supervise what I see and whom I meet. Secondly, they are to keep an eye on the contacts I do make so that if any of them get out of line they can be dealt with later. Thirdly, they are to misrepresent my questions and misinterpret the answers. I approach a group of people and ask the interpreter to ask them if they love the Communist government. He turns to them and utters a stream of what, to me, is unintelligible gibberish. They answer in a similar vein. He turns to me and says, "They love Communism with all their hearts." The only difficulty is that I have no way of knowing what he asked them or what they said in reply. He may have said, "He wants to know what you had for breakfast." They may have said, "You know very well that we didn't have any breakfast." Since he is a devoted Communist, utterly dedicated to the interests of the Party, it is highly improbable that he will repeat anything that reflects badly upon it.

Ninety-nine out of a hundred people who visit Russia and come back to tell their friends and acquaintances all about it are in exactly the same position I would be in if I went. They have no way of knowing how much of what they have been told is really true. The tragic part is that most of them do not realize this. They quote authoritatively what they have been told by the Communist interpreter as the objective truth.

A well known businessman, a prominent clergyman, or a politician goes to Russia for a brief tour. On his return he is met by representatives of the press at the airport where he gives his impressions of the present mood of the Russian masses. He is whisked off to a radio station where he discusses the changes that have occurred in the personal relationships of the Presidium of the Communist Party. He may even appear on television where he talks at some length about the present attitude of the Red Army towards their Communist masters. The only people who are bigger idiots than he are those who take any notice of what he says. By the very nature of things, he can be nothing but an unconscious agent of Communist propaganda. He can report only what he saw and heard. What he saw was limited and superficial, and what he heard was channeled to him through the Communist Party.

It has been well said, "A fool learns by his own experience; a wise man learns by the experience of others." The major portion of our knowledge is gained through the means of communication. In Russia these are completely controlled by the Communist Party. Every newspaper is a Communist propaganda sheet. All radio and television programs are designed to convey messages selected by the Communist Party. Every textbook, every novel, every play and movie is designed to advance the ideas approved by the Party. Thus information which is the raw material of thought is fed to the Russian people by the Communists. Public opinion in Russia is carefully molded by the Communist Party.

If a tourist realizes the serious limitations of his situation, in certain specialized fields, he can obtain valid information from his trip. For example, he can secure clear information about the Russian boast that they have equalized the status of women. Their boast is quite justified. Americans do not really treat their women with equality. They do not allow them, for example, to mine coal or to perform heavy manual work on the roads. Such tasks are kept solely for men. There is no such bourgeois discrimination in Russia, and tourists to Russia may observe that this is so. One tourist told me that when he came out of a theatre at eleven o'clock at night he saw a group of old grandmothers working in the rain laying blacktop on the roads. As he travels in the train, the tourist may see women swinging their picks in the railway gangs, usually under the supervision of a male fore-man. Such things a tourist may see, but to secure a genuine insight into the minds and feelings of the people is an impossibility in the situation existing in Russia.

Discussing this with some wide-eyed innocents recently returned from Russia, I made the statement that tourists returning from behind the Iron Curtain are very frequently instruments of Communist propaganda. They were horrified at the suggestion. As we continued in conversation, one of the women commented on the encouraging progress being made by Russian Baptists. Said she, "They now have seven thousand churches."

"Here is the very kind of thing to which I was referring," I replied. "You are unconsciously giving Communist propaganda."

"I resent that very much," she said.

"Let's consider your statement," I said. "You tell me that there are seven thousand Baptist churches. How do you know?"

She mentioned the name of a friend of hers as the source of her information.

"And how does he know?"

"He knows the Baptist preacher in Moscow and has known him for years," was the reply.

"I know one of the Baptist preachers here in Los Angeles and have known him for years. Were I to go to him and ask how many Baptist churches there are in California, what would he do? He'd pull down a Baptist yearbook, seek the information, and give me the answer for the different Baptist segments. Somebody has to take the statistics. Who do you suppose took these statistics that you are giving me?"

She said, "I don't know."

"The Communists took them, of course. Whether they are true or false, we have not the faintest idea."

No tourist of Russia can get any idea whatsoever of the strength of Baptist work in Russia. All he can do is to go and see one or two Baptist churches, usually those in Moscow or Leningrad. When Bob Pierce, President of World Vision, was in Kiev, he asked the guide to show him the Baptist church there. The guide was at a loss. Tourists do not ask to visit the Baptist church in Kiev. They go only in Moscow and Leningrad. In the city of Kiev which has a population of a million people, she did not know where a Baptist church was to be found. By the following day, however, she had discovered one. It consisted of a mere handful of people meeting in a house. When we consider that the Protestants of Russia are all in these Baptist churches, the complacency of Christians is appalling.

The statistics regarding the strength of Baptist work in Russia vary greatly from time to time. When the leaders from the Russian Baptists toured America about 1955, they quoted the number of Baptists then in Russia as being three million. In 1959, the number was given as five hundred thousand. Either the Baptists in Russia backslid greatly in those few years, or someone manipulated the statistics.

In Indianapolis, I spoke to the farm editor of the television station who was about to visit Russia. I told him that he would come back a propagandist for the Communists. He replied, "I know I will. How can I help it?"

"Oh, that's easy," I said. "As soon as you get there, overthrow the Communist government and re-establish freedom of speech, freedom of movement, freedom of the press, and freedom of communication. Abolish all the psychological inhibitions Communism has produced in the people during their rule of forty years. Then go round and dig under every child's playground and see what you find."

In the Ukraine, the Germans were welcomed by the Ukrainians as liberators In the city of Vinnitza there were discovered mass graves of ten thousand bodies. Over some of these graves the Communists had built Parks of Culture and Rest including a child's playground and a sporting arena. A tourist going there at normal times would see nothing except excellent recreational facilities for the citizens and particularly for the children.

Delegations are the source of dangerous delusions indeed. What we see with our eyes is limited. Observation is no substitute for understanding. A man can learn more about Communism in an hour by taking a book like *How to be a Good Communist* by Liu Shao-chi or *Problems of Leninism* by Stalin than he can in a year as a tourist who sees nothing but what the Communists show him. Observation may be minutely accurate and interpretation completely erroneous.

A visitor went on a tour of a tuberculosis sanitarium. He walked through the grounds, first of all, and there he was greatly impressed by the well kept lawns and the beautiful landscaped gardens. Upon entering the building, he was met by a charming receptionist who smiled at him warmly and took him on a tour of the sanitarium.

In the spotless kitchen, he found the finest cooking equipment he had ever seen. He examined the plumbing and found it exceptional in quality and efficiency.

After duly admiring the facilities of the institution, he was escorted into the wards. In preparation for his coming, the patients had all been given a dose of anti-pertussive mixture, otherwise known as cough syrup. The peaceful atmosphere was not disturbed by undue coughing. The patients were propped up neatly on snowy white pillows. Many of them had a becoming flush on their cheeks. Hovering around were nurses who were giving them personal attention far better than any service available in the best hotel. When mealtime arrived, each patient was served with tasty food which had been carefully prepared and attractively served on individual trays.

When his tour was ended, the visitor was duly impressed by all he had seen. Said he, "There are many good features about tuberculosis, features which are at least equal, if not superior to the features of a healthy life. The patient lives in an environment of cleanliness and beauty. He has economic security. He does not need to rise at six o'clock each morning to battle his way through the teeming traffic and compete in the struggle to earn a living. Food, clothing, and shelter are all provided. Every need is supplied by attentive young female nurses. He has reached the goal of economic security for which we all strive. I think that the dangers of tuberculosis are grossly exaggerated. We can at least co-exist with it."

Hearing this, some puzzled person might turn to him and say, "But what about the tuberculosis germ?"

"I didn't see one."

"Did you look?"

"Of course I looked. I looked everywhere—in the drawers, under the beds, behind the doors, everywhere—and I swear I did not see a single tuberculosis germ. I don't believe they exist."

Suppose that such a report was made by a medical man who had been trained to know that what he saw was merely superficial, and that out of human sight was an evil, pathological organism doing its fearful work; who should have known that behind the apparent calm, there was a world of agony and racking coughs which would cause the patients to spit up their lungs in pus and blood and would send them to their deaths. A medical man who made a report like that would be judged criminally insane.

Preachers should be physicians in the realm of the spirit as medical men are in the realm of the body. When preachers report only the superficial things they see, and, by inference, minimize the gravity of the germ of godlessness, they betray their responsibility as Christian leaders. The tragedy is that they do it all unwittingly.

A preacher visited Russia in 1938. He saw some splendid new buildings going up, and he reported that Russia was fulfilling the kingdom of God on earth. What was going on at that time was horrible to imagine. It was the period of the great Stalinist purges, when Stalin was watering the soil of Russia with the blood of the Communist elite. As a visitor, the clergyman did not see one execution or one trial. He saw only magnificent new buildings and on the basis of this he made his report. Seeing without understanding is the certain pathway of delusion.

Seeing is not necessarily believing. If seeing is believing, you cannot tell me anything about American football because I have seen it with my own eyes. I want to describe to you what I saw.

If you do not believe me, I am prepared to go into any court in the land and swear under oath that this is what I saw.

It was in Los Angeles at the Coliseum. The University of Southern California was playing the University of California in a home-coming match. It was a magnificent spectacle. A hundred thousand people were gathered together. A hundred thousand people is a huge crowd. They must be entertained because the devil finds work for idle hands to do. Clowns have always been found to be very entertaining, so with typical American genius the organizers hit upon a remarkable scheme. They dressed all the football players up like clowns. They put them in the most ridiculous and grotesque garments I have ever seen. They were padded and patted in every direction like an Eskimo bride at a winter wedding breakfast. They had baggy pants. They protruded at the rear and at the knees. They wore enormous helmets with protruding jaws. It was the funniest looking sight I had ever seen.

About fifty of these clowns ran on to the playing field and a strange thing happened. Instead of bursting out laughing as would have been quite natural, everybody began clapping and cheering. I admit bewilderment at this incomprehensible manifestation of American psychology. After these clowns had run around throwing the ball to one another for ten or fifteen minutes, most of them became weary or bored and went to sit down on some benches at the side of the field. Eleven clowns remained on each side of the line running across the middle of the playing field, and seven of them knelt down opposite one another and started to pray. When they had said their prayers, one of them flicked the ball back to a guy standing behind. He apparently took a liking to it, and thought he would take it home, so he cut across that field like a streak of lightning. The others saw what he was doing and rushed after him. He swerved and he weaved. He approached the sideline. It looked as though he was going to get away. But suddenly, hurtling through the air came a massive body which crashed into him and knocked him right over. This was rather cruel, but maybe it was fair enough since he was trying to steal the ball like that.

At this point nobody seemed to know quite what to do. A clown in a costume all of his own with up and down stripes which made him look like a convict blew a whistle and the game stopped. One side called a committee meeting. What took place at this committee meeting, I do not know exactly. One thing they did was to interchange a few of the clowns who had apparently grown tired in the struggle.

They resumed with another session of prayer. I feel that this recurrent prayer in American football is one of the hopeful signs of the day. When the center man flicked the ball back to the one standing behind him, he played them a dirty trick. In all my living days, I have never seen a dirtier deed. How he had the gall to do it before two hundred thousand staring eyes, I will never know. Right in the middle of the game, he changed his side. Instead of running forward, he turned and ran round backwards. When he had gone back about ten yards, however, someone caught him and knocked him over. Wasn't that a dirty trick to change his side in the middle of the game like that? I know he did. I saw him with my own eyes.

You say to me, "Oh, you're crazy! That man hadn't changed his side at all. He'd gone back to get in a good position to make a forward pass and they trapped him." You know this because you know the rules of the game. You know its purposes and you know its motives. You are in tune with its spirit. But if you knew none of these things, if you came, as I do, from another land where the rules for football are quite different, where the game has no forward pass, and if you took the rules which were familiar to you and interpreted what you saw in terms of them you would be apt to make conclusions very similar to those which I reached.

When we observe what the Communists do without knowing the rules of the game, without knowing Communist doctrine, morality, objectives, and methods, when we project upon them our own basic Christian standards, our conclusions are as ridiculous as my interpretation of an American football match. They are far more dangerous. There must be assiduous study of the doctrines of Communism if the necessary understanding of their psychology, morality, and program is to be achieved. There is no substitute for knowledge. Ignorance is evil and paralytic.

The greatest ally Communism has is the existing ignorance concerning its true nature. War must be declared on this ignorance.

IX

BRAINWASHING

THE WORD "brainwashing" is a very recent addition to the English language. A new word was necessary because it signified an experience that was previously unknown. Since its introduction it has passed into common speech and is used routinely by large numbers of people, many of whom have only the vaguest idea of its meaning. In many cases it is used to describe processes that have existed for centuries, and its specific meaning has, to a large degree, been lost. But the phenomenon of brainwashing is one of the more frightening developments of the twentieth century. It is an accurate and destructive science. It is an assault upon the human mind itself. The Communists have proved they can distort the human mind as the torturers of history distorted the body.

An American girl went to China as a Fulbright scholar. She was not a Communist, but neither was she an active anti-Communist. After studying for a year or so in Communist China, she was arrested and underwent various mysterious treatments. At the end of this treatment, she confessed that she had gone to China as an imperialist spy, and professed profound repentance for her treachery. She was then allowed to go free.

As she crossed into Hong Kong, she was met by newspaper reporters, and a remarkable story unfolded. She told the reporters she had been a vicious spy on behalf of the American imperialists. Her attitude was a composite of guilt and self-loathing, mingled with hatred of her own country and a passionate love for the Chinese Communists. She was almost lyrical in her gratitude and devotion to her captors. She described how wonderful they were. She had deserved to die, but they had spared her life. In their hands she had been born again. To them she owed an eternal debt of gratitude for the new life she now lived.

The reporters questioned her about her treatment in prison. Had not her feet been in chains? Oh, yes, her feet had been in chains, but what loving, kind, wonderful people the Communists were. Was it not true that her hands had been handcuffed behind her back? Yes, her hands had been handcuffed behind her back, but they had treated her with absolute kindness and wonderful love.

What were the experiences which had brought about this remarkable situation where she believed she had done things she had not done, felt guilt for crimes she had not committed, and loved with a passionate intensity those who had tortured and tormented her? We see in this young woman an end product of the phenomenon known as brainwashing.

A young man joined the armed forces of his country and crossed the sea to fight in Korea. Early in the Korean War, he was taken prisoner by the Communists. He very soon confessed that he had engaged in germ warfare. While in the hands of the Communists, he fell ill and was transferred back to America at operation "Little Switch"—the interchange of sick prisoners. Upon his return, he needed to be institutionalized. In the institution he sat squat-legged in his cell in the grip of a profound, irreducible melancholy, with a tendency towards self-destruction. He was in love with his mistress, Death. This young soldier is a second example of the results of brainwashing.

The word is sometimes used to describe the experience, on a mass scale, of American prisoners in the hands of the Chinese Communists. America has fought in a number of wars in which prisoners have been taken. Such prisoners always proved a thorn in the side of their captors. They were very difficult to control, they were courageous, they were subject to the discipline of their officers in the prison, they were gripped with a comradely devotion to their fellow prisoners, and they made numerous attempts at escape. When American prisoners of war fell into the hands of the Communists, however, a disturbing transformation occurred. They were reduced to a selfish, un-co-ordinated rabble without discipline or unity. Informing on one another was the order of the day. A handful of Communist Chinese kept large groups of American prisoners under control without brutal bashings, without barbed wire entanglements, and with little apparent difficulty. Of many thousands of prisoners, not one made any attempt to escape during the entire period of the imprisonment. Only a small segment were able to withstand completely the attempts of the Communists to indoctrinate them. Another small group became openly pro-Communist. The remainder were demoralized. Forty per cent of them died. The Turkish prisoners, on the other hand, maintained an excellent record. Their discipline was held completely from top to bottom. Not one Turkish prisoner died, and not one collaborated.

So concerned were the American authorities that they instituted an inquiry to seek the causes of this revolution in the conduct of American prisoners. A team of trained medical officers examined the prisoners, collected details of the treatment they had received, and probed for the causes of this debacle. This evidence was published in the book, *In Every War but One.*[1] Their findings were alarming indeed. In an effort to prevent similar occurrences in the future, the army sought to establish a code of conduct for any soldier so unfortunate as to fall into the hands of the Communists in the future. The Communist assault on the human mind is historically unique and alarming in its effectiveness.

To understand the rationale of this attack we need to understand the Communist concept of the mind itself. The Communists are complete materialists. They believe that matter in motion is the sum total of all being, that there is nothing in the uni-

---

[1] Eugene Kinkead, *In Every War but One,* W. W. Norton & Co., New York, 1959.

verse but matter in motion. Man is a material machine. Within his body a stomach secretes gastric juice, a liver secretes bile, a brain secretes emotion and thought.

A materialist scientist built a mechanical dog which he kept in a room in his home. When he opened the door and allowed the light to shine on the eyes of the dog, it moved forward and growled. When he shut the door, it moved back into position. If he stroked the dog along the back, it wagged its tail. If he tickled it underneath, it lay down. Said the scientist, "The only difference between this dog and my pet dog that runs, jumps, barks, and comes with me when I take a walk is one of degree. There is no difference in kind."

The Communists go further. The only difference between the mechanical dog, the living dog, and the human being is one of degree. There is no difference in kind. The human body is simply a material machine. It is as automatic as an automobile. Man is a complex of conditioned behavior. The machinery is very complex, particularly the brain which is so complex that it gives the impression of freedom, choice, and volition. But thought is merely a reflection of certain electronic impulses within the brain. The Communists, therefore, believe that if they can understand brain structure, the building up of brain patterns and brain circuits, they will be able to understand the formation of human thought and will be able to control and direct human thought.

The functional unit within the brain is the conditioned reflex. The Communists have studied the formation, control and elimination of conditioned reflexes. A reflex is an unlearned muscular response to a natural or unconditioned stimulus. At birth a baby has certain remarkable skills. For example, it can cry, and crying is a complex mechanical process requiring the co-ordination of a number of groups of muscles. Again, a baby can suck. These muscular skills are the external manifestations of certain inborn brain patterns. They are unconditioned reflex actions.

At birth, the process of development and learning begins. Learning is the accumulation of new brain patterns leading to muscular co-ordination of a more complex nature. The baby is taken and laid in a basinette over which is suspended a little colored ball. The little hands strike at the ball. At first the movements are un-co-ordinated and multi-directional, but gradually skill is acquired until at length the little hand can hit the ball at will. The skill is revealed in co-ordinated muscular activity, but the controlling mechanism is the pattern that has been developed within the brain. The skill is a conditioned reflex.

As experience continues, the baby learns to sit up, to walk, to talk, to write, to ride a bicycle, to play the piano, to use a typewriter, to drive an automobile. All these skills are conditioned reflexes. Experience shows itself in intricate patterns of muscular activity, but the real pattern is established within the brain.

The Communists believe that the mind is simply a complex of conditioned reflexes, and that if they can understand the techniques by which these conditioned reflexes are built up and how they can be broken down, they have acquired mastery over the mind itself.

The great scientist who studied the conditioned reflex thoroughly and systematically was the Russian, Pavlov. He began his scientific experiments under the rule of the Czar. Lenin early realized the vast significance of Pavlov's studies for the Communist program of changing the entire mental outlook of the Russian people. Pavlov was therefore given favored treatment by the Communist regime.

The experimental animal that he used was the dog. The basic reflex that he studied was the salivary reflex. When a dog is hungry and is shown some meat, his mouth waters. The sight or the smell of the meat is the normal stimulus for the flow of saliva. In preparation for this experiment, Pavlov operated on these dogs and introduced a tube into the salivary duct to divert the saliva from the intestinal tract into a bottle so that its flow could be measured. When the dogs were hungry, he showed them meat and the saliva flowed. The next step was to associate the ringing of a bell with the viewing of the meat and the flowing of the saliva. At first he rang a bell at the same time as he showed them the meat. Then he rang the bell a few seconds before he showed them the meat. In this way, the ringing of the bell was associated with the normal stimulus in such a way that the ringing of the bell itself was sufficient to start the salivary flow. Gradually the time interval was extended until, finally, the dogs were so conditioned that whenever the bell rang, the saliva flowed. The flowing of the saliva in this situation was a conditioned reflex. The ringing bell was the artificial stimulus that produced the reflex response.

Pavlov experimented with a large range of stimuli to reflex action. He took colored lights that moved in a circular pattern, lights that moved in an elliptical pattern, and, after due training and conditioning, was able to obtain specific responses for each of the lights that he showed. He subjected the dogs to contradictory stimuli and studied their behavior to see which reflexes were more powerful. He had a whole kennel of dogs each of which was conditioned to react to a given stimulus in a fixed manner.

In 1924 Leningrad experienced a major flood. Pavlov's dogs were trapped and, for several days, were cut off from human help. When finally they were rescued, their muzzles were just sticking out of the water. For several days, they had been cold, frightened, hungry, and exhausted. After their rescue, the acute observer, Pavlov, noticed a strange thing. Some of his dogs went into a state of profound canine depression. They lost interest in food, and in the normal activities of a dog's life. There was no barking and no rushing about. Their movements were slow and infrequent. To them life seemed to have lost its luster. Most interesting of all was the fact that in this state their conditioned reflexes were abolished. Pavlov found that he could then condition them according to an entirely different pattern.

Pavlov applied the information thus accidentally discovered to experiments to destroy conditioned reflex patterns. At first he continued to experiment with dogs but during the last ten years of his life, man became his experimental animal. He developed techniques which could shatter the established pattern of human personality so that the fragments could be integrated into a new structure of memory, judgment, and emotion in line with the desires of the Communist craftsmen.

The first step in the process was to bring about a state of breakdown similar to that experienced by the dogs. Pavlov called it cortical inhibition of the higher cerebral function. This is the state commonly known as a mental breakdown which has occurred naturally in humans for many years. Pavlov established techniques whereby he could cause an artificial mental breakdown. The four things necessary to bring about this state were present in the breakdown of the trapped dogs. They are exhaustion, confusion, chronic physical pain, and emotional tension or fear.

EXHAUSTION

To parody a statement of Tolstoi: "Whom the Communists wish to brainwash, they first exhaust." The first step, then, is to exhaust the individual. He is subjected to long periods of wakefulness. Various tactics are adopted to make sure that he cannot rest. He may have to snatch brief periods of sleep with a light shining in his face. If he turns over, the attendant comes along and awakens him with a command to get back into position. Sleep is short and sporadic. The techniques to induce prolonged wakefulness may vary from pleasurable, continuous excitement, to physical pain. The essential feature is to rob the body of sleep so that utter exhaustion prevails.

CONFUSION

With exhaustion, there is the concurrent development of confusion. While the defenses of his mind are weakened and undermined by his extreme weariness, the patient is subjected to lengthy periods of questioning. He sits facing his interrogator. A bright light shines relentlessly into his eyes. Questions are asked one after the other. There is no attorney present to warn him against loaded questions. There is no privilege of refraining from answering for fear of possible self-incrimination. Every question must be answered. At first the questions are simple. They often concern his social origin, early childhood and family. The questioner often shows a conciliatory attitude. Gradually the questions pry deeper and deeper into the hidden recesses of his mind. Questions are framed in such a way that any simple answer contains a damaging admission. Questions relative to imaginary crimes he is alleged to have committed are subtly introduced.

One of the most frequent accusations made against missionaries in China was that they operated secret radio transmitters to broadcast the fruits of their espionage to Chiang Kai-shek or to America. The questioner might suddenly ask, "Are you sorry now that you transmitted this information?" If he answers simply "Yes," or "No," he is admitting association with a "transmitter."

If the mind is alert, the trap is seen and avoided, but this requires clear insight and lucid expression. As exhaustion develops, the defenses of the mind break down. A question containing a trap is asked; a simple answer is given; and the subject is caught. After a few more questions, they confront him with the hidden admission contained in the simple answer he gave. He denies it. They take him back to his original answer and ask, "Isn't this what you said?" He replies that this is so.

"Well, does this not acknowledge so and so?" He has to admit that it does.

Relentlessly they continue. "Previously you acknowledged this; now you deny it. When were you lying, then or now?" He insists that he is speaking the truth now.

"If you were a liar then, how can we believe you now?" they demand. He becomes so confused that the borderline of truth and falsehood becomes blurred. The connection between reality and fantasy is lost and he is no longer sure what is true and what it false. In such a condition, he becomes an easy prey for the suggestion of the Communist brainwashing therapist.

CHRONIC PHYSICAL PAIN

Along with exhaustion and confusion, the "brainwashee" is subject to chronic physical pain. This is applied with great care for their goal is always clearly before them. They are not aiming at torturing their victim till he confesses to something he knows to be untrue. They desire to reduce him to the state where he believes the untruth to be true. They do not want a physical breakdown before they get a mental one. Physical damage should not be permanent or leave clearly visible scars. The physical pain, therefore, is chronic in nature, and not acute torture. If the weather is cold, the victim may be left without adequate covering so that hands and feet become frostbitten. He may be made to endure hunger and thirst. Chronic sores may break out. He may be left in a position of extreme discomfort, unable to stand up and unable to sit or lie down. Physical movement may be restricted by handcuffs or chains. He longs and prays for an end to his apparently endless ordeal.

FEAR

In addition to exhaustion, confusion, and chronic physical pain, there is the constant application of emotional tension or fear. The emotional personality is analyzed to determine the weakest point. If there is intense devotion to wife or family, threats to them may be held constantly before the victim's eyes. A group may inhabit a cell. One by one they are called out at intervals of a few days. The sound of a shot is heard. The man taken out does not return. Anxiety and fear are experienced by those who remain. Each lives in constant inner emotional torment. By such processes as these, a mental breakdown is induced. The old personality pattern is shattered and the victim is ready to be molded according to the desires of the Communist Party.

Exhaustion, confusion, chronic physical pain and emotional tension, employed in scientific balance, finally achieve the first goal. A breakdown occurs. The mind fragments. In Pavlovian language, cortical inhibition of the higher cerebral function occurs.

The characteristics of this breakdown are as follows.

1. *Physical retardation.* The victim tends to remain almost motionless in the same position for long periods of time. Movements when they do take place are slow and ponderous. There is a total lack of vitality, interest and enthusiasm.

2. *Memory fragmentation.* The integrated pattern of past experience embracing memory, interpretation and judgment is shattered. Fragments of past experience are remembered dimly but without relation to other memories of events. The time sequence of events is lost. The borderline between fact and fancy, between memory and dream is blurred.

3. *Melancholy.* The typical pattern is one of deep melancholia. The mind is gripped by a nameless woe. There is deep and enduring depression. Frequently suicidal tendencies develop as the misery appears too heavy to be borne. If the physical means are available, the sufferer will readily end his own life.

4. *Increased suggestibility.* The barriers of the mind are down. Memory is faded. Logic is impaired. Judgment is impossible. In the absence of the restraints of the healthy mind, the power of suggestion is enhanced.

The Communists take advantage of this weak and unresisting state, and, by suggestion, link the shattered fragments of memory into the new pattern. They suggest the new ideas which they want believed. To these ideas they attach the sense of guilt which the victim is already feeling. They remove the excess emotional depression and then identify themselves with measures to alleviate his suffering, but they are careful to leave the delusional beliefs unaltered. They now have their end product—a person with memories of things he has not done, with a sense of guilt for crimes he did not commit, and with a passionate love for those who have persecuted and tormented him.

Suggestion is a powerful force even under normal conditions. This has been discovered by advertisers and used to considerable advantage. I myself have frequently carried out an interesting little experiment on the power of suggestion. One of the problems confronting me in my itinerant life is that perfectly well-meaning, hospitable Americans try to persuade me to drink that dark, viscous, bitter beverage called coffee. Sometimes I drink it, but sometimes I say: "I used to drink it, but I carried out some research and discovered what coffee really is. Do you know what it really is? They take the castor oil bean, soak it in shellac until it is thoroughly impregnated. They put on a great advertising racket and pretend that it comes from Brazil so that they can treble the price. They grind it up and they brew it. The castor oil gives it the flavor, the shellac gives it the color, and the idiots drink it." It is amazing how many people have looked at me with wide open eyes and said: "Is that true?" No matter how stupid the statement, if it is made with an attitude of apparent sincerity and conviction, there are always those who will be convinced of its truth.

Once people are conditioned so that a certain word is associated with emotions of repulsion or anger, that word becomes a trigger by which those emotions may be discharged. Reason and logic are quite unnecessary. That word is used, the trigger is pulled, and out come the emotions. This was brought home to me very powerfully one evening when I was speaking upon the subject of brainwashing at a church. I used my illustration about coffee to indicate how suggestible people are. I reached the climax: the castor oil gives it the flavor, the shellac gives it the color, and the idiots drink it. To my great surprise, the whole audience broke out into loud, sustained applause. I was startled. I had thought I was telling a joke. Suddenly the truth dawned on me. The audience consisted of a group of coffee haters. This was a group to whom drinking coffee was a sin. They did not examine my argument critically; they responded to the trigger. The word became a stimulus to a reflex response. Once people are conditioned like that, there is no need for logic, reason or truth. All that is needed is for the word to be said and out will come the emotions.

The Communists have taken the words "Capitalism," "American imperialism," and even the word "peace" and made them trigger words and used them in slogans. "Capitalism" immediately conjures up a picture of greed and exploitation, and releases emotions of scorn and anger. "American imperialism," attached to the most altruistic American actions, makes them appear shabby and shameful. The word "peace," associated with Communist treachery, brutality and tyranny, clothes Communism in garments of hope and beauty. To these trigger words, young people throughout the world are being conditioned to respond.

This campaign of the Communists has been so successful that even the most ardent supporters of Capitalism hesitate to use the word and search for some less offensive synonym. It needs to be constantly taught that Capitalism has produced a standard of economic well-being and simultaneously sustained individual liberty to a degree unapproached by any other system. Capitalism is a dynamic system that can adjust to changing conditions and it is infinitely preferable to the tyranny of regimentation under the dictatorship of a self-proclaimed elite, whether this latter system calls itself "Communism" or some more euphemistic name.

Let us return to our victim undergoing brainwashing. He has reached the point of mental breakdown with fragmentation of mind and memory. By a process of suggestion, the Communists link together the shattered fragments of their victim's mind. Certain memories they carefully retain. Others they deliberately confuse and eliminate. A missionary serving with the China Inland Mission when the Communists took over China underwent the experience of brainwashing. He tells how they convinced him that under every church that he had built he constructed a storeroom for ammunition for Chiang Kai-shek's soldiers. It was true that he had built a room under each church where he had been. This room was the baptistry for the baptism of adults by immersion. When the Communists had him thoroughly exhausted, depressed and confused, they filled these rooms with weapons and showed them to him. They had him handle the weapons and ammunition. Later on, they took his finger prints from the ammunition that he had handled in these rooms and used them to convince him that he had built the rooms and filled them with weapons for the use of the forces of Chiang Kai-shek. He remembered building the rooms, and he remembered handling the weapons. By clever suggestion, the Communists were able to weave these scraps of memory together and to convince him of the truth of their accusations. He was then overwhelmed with guilt for his treacherous acts.

After the experience of brainwashing, the victim suffers from severe emotional depression. The excessive elements of this depression are removed in various ways. They allow time to do its healing work. It is possible that they use electric shock treatment. The advantage of shock treatment is that it can remove emotional depression without affecting the ideas associated with the depression. If an individual is convinced that his grandmother left him a million dollars and that his wicked step-sister stole it from him, he is likely to be exceedingly miserable in his delusional state. After shock treatment, he remains convinced that his grandmother left him the million dollars and that his wicked step-sister stole it from him, but can now face this fact with a measure of equanimity. Moreover, shock treatment is followed by an amnesia, and there is no memory of the treatment's being received. It could be given privately and the individual would never remember that he had received it.

In time, the victim of brainwashing is brought out and presented in court. He makes his confession. He is observed and interviewed by the reporters. No apparent physical damage is noted, and his confession goes out to all the world.

It is possible to recover from brainwashing just as recovery is possible in cases of mental collapse induced by the pressures of society. For a cure to be effected, the victim must be removed from the environment containing the pressures that produced the collapse. The missionary who believed himself guilty of building ammunition storerooms in the churches was kept quiet in a dark room, after his release from China, and allowed to talk. As he released his tensions, the real became disassociated from the false, and he returned to a normal mental and spiritual state. Most people do recover, but not all. In any case, the scars of their ordeal remain.

INDOCTRINATION

The term "brainwashing" is not always used to indicate the process described. The word has captured public imagination and is used very loosely. The process of indoctrination by repetition rather than reason is frequently termed brainwashing. The Communists are adept at this also. They tell a lie, make it big, repeat it often, and the majority of people believe them.

This, of course, is a principle which has long been practised by advertisers. There are some particularly remarkable examples in the field of tobacco advertising. There is little attempt at a reasoned, logical argument. They seek a catchy slogan to repeat over and over again. Some years ago when a certain company was promoting an especially long cigarette, the slogan adopted was: "Screens out irritants but never screens out flavor." The idea apparently was that the length of the cigarette acted as a filter. The question which should arise at once is: What happens when the cigarette burns down to the normal size? Yet this obvious lack of logic and common sense apparently made no difference to the effectiveness of the advertising campaign. The slogan was repeated so many times that large numbers of people unquestionably assumed its truth.

Driving back one night from Milwaukee to Chicago, I listened to a remarkable interview on the radio. The man being interviewed was a prosecuting attorney. He was discussing drinking drivers. He was devastating. He said, "Anyone who drinks and drives an automobile is a potential murderer. Anyone who drinks, drives an automobile and kills is an actual murderer. There is no difference between killing as a result of drunken driving, and killing with a gun. Since everybody drives, nobody should drink. One drink lowers your efficiency and increases your reaction time. There is only one place for drinking drivers and that is prison. By God's grace, that's where I intend to put them!"

No sooner had he finished than the announcer's voice was heard: "The foregoing interview was sponsored by a well-known brand of beer." There followed a specious statement that since this beer was the best of all beers, you owed it to yourself and your friends to pick up a carton of it on the way home and to keep it in the refrigerator as you never knew when your friends might drive by and call on you. If you did not have a drink there to welcome them, you were certainly a poor host and no gentleman.

The sponsors of this program were not trying to ruin their business. They doubtless knew very well that the program would do them no harm, for they were well aware that repetition would conquer reason. The listening audience would hear the prosecuting attorney once, and perhaps they would agree with him; but they would hear the beer announcement a hundred times. Reason may reach the conscious mind while repetition influences the unconscious mind which is the source of so much human conduct.

The Communists know that if they want something accepted without question, they must say it, say it, and say it again. Therefore they are repeating day and night by radio, by television, by literature of every type, two simple lies: one is that wherever Communism is in power, the people are prosperous, healthy, happy and free; the other is that America is vile and evil beyond measure, a land of hunger, malnutrition, depression, exploitation, poverty and fear, and a desperate threat to the peace of the world. An evidence of this Communist technique is a book which they have published in Australia called *This is America*. There is not one word in this book which is not quoted directly from the non-Communist American press. Out of the tremendous quantity of material published, the Communists have taken any statement which can help to build a picture of a poverty-ridden, oppressed America. All the articles and statements that suggest otherwise, they have ignored completely. The following are some quotations from the book.

> "One third of the city's babies, born and unborn, suffer from malnutrition as a result of high prices, the Right Rev. Charles K. Gilbert, Bishop of the Episcopal Diocese of New York, told the Congressional Committee." New York *World Telegram*, September 25, 1947.

> "We feed our hogs better than our children." Heading on an article in the *American Magazine*, October, 1947, by Fred Bailey, Executive Director of National Agricultural Research, Inc.

> "Approximately 2,500,000 residents of New York face undernourishment and deficiency diets due to the inflated costs of food. This is the grim, outstanding evidence produced by a four-day hearing on food prices by the eastern sub-committee of a joint Congressional Committee." Quoted in the *Christian Science Monitor*, September 26, 1947.

> "Three fourths of the nation's children suffer from undernourishment, a study of Pennsylvania State College established." Quoted by *Associated Press* on December 20, 1950.

The Communists do not need to tell lies in order to create the picture they desire. All they need to do is to select from the total picture those things that fit into their pre-conceived pattern. As Tennyson said:

> *A lie that's half a truth is the wickedest lie of all,*
> *For a lie that's all a lie can be met with and fought*
> *   outright,*
> *But a lie that is half a truth is a harder matter to*
> *   fight.*

The Communists are creating a picture of America which is completely false and are projecting this picture into the minds of the people of the world. What America does or does not do makes little difference to this picture. It is easy to say, "Let the facts speak for themselves." Unfortunately facts have a very soft voice, and their message is not heard by those who are not in the immediate environment. The United States-Canadian border is a fact. The absence of military establishments, the frequency and ease of two-way transportation are indisputable facts. They have not been able to contradict for millions of people the constantly reiterated Communist lie that the United States is viciously imperialistic, threatening the peace and integrity of all the people of the world.

In the formation of public opinion, it is not what you do that counts, but what people believe you do. Opinions vary concerning the wisdom of the action of President Eisenhower in sending troops into Little Rock, Arkansas, in September, 1958. The fact is indisputable that they were sent in to enable Negro children to attend school. However, competent observers report that the majority of people in Africa believe that they were sent in to prevent Negro children from attending school. The attitude of these people towards America is formed from their erroneous beliefs, not from the facts. The Communists spare no expenses and make prodigious efforts to print and distribute literature giving a completely false picture of life and character in the United States. The falsity of this picture of America is only surpassed by the picture they present of alleged universal happiness and contentment under Communism.

The difference between life under Communist rule and life in America is well illustrated by the fact that whenever Communism comes to power, in spite of the glory of their promises, the fearful reality proves the magnitude of their deception and people flee by the million. At every Communist border in the world where there is any possibility of escape, this exodus continues. The United States, on the other hand, is a magnet to her neighbors. A million people a year risk their lives not trying to get out, but trying to get in, not to live at the highest standard, but at the lowest standard. Great numbers cross the Rio Grande River and enter illegally from Mexico. Conditions in Mexico are certainly very poor, but this alone would not account for the influx. Conditions in Turkey are far from ideal. Poverty there is rife also. Yet there is no stream of refugees from Turkey into Russia. These facts must be told till they are known in every nook and cranny of the earth. America should mobilize her remarkable skill with the means of communication to achieve this end. The alternative is to become an island of unease in a surrounding sea of hatred.

The phenomenon of brainwashing is one of the manifestations of the true nature of Communism. It is rebellion against God; it is rebellion against the human mind; it is rebellion against the purpose, significance and value of the individual. The way to defeat it is to defeat the program of Communist expansion. When the door closes behind you in the brainwashing chamber, it will be too late.

X

THE DIFFICULT, DEVIOUS
AND DANGEROUS DIALECTIC

THE DIALECTICAL PHILOSOPHY is the most difficult, the least understood, and possibly the most important aspect of Communism. It is this philosophy which directs the apparently unpredictable and constantly changing Communist course.

Most people are very practical. They believe the evidence of their senses. They look for an enemy which is obvious and tangible. They say, "I am interested in the Communists, and concerned by their actions. Tell me who they are and show me where they are and I will know how to act." Or they may say, "I am interested in Communist economic theory, in their military power and in their subversive organization, but don't talk to me about philosophy. That is too deep for me. Talking about their philosophy only confuses me." Such people are interested in the superficial manifestations of Communist organization, but they are not interested in the philosophic credo from which they draw their motivating forces, their basic strategy, and their confidence in the future. They are reminiscent of dairy farmers who are interested in milk, but not in cows, orchardists who are interested in fruit, but not in trees, or apiarists who are interested in honey but not in bees. The superficial manifestations of Communism are inseparably related to its underlying philosophic concept.

145

As I have travelled throughout this country addressing civic clubs, patriotic groups, churches and schools, I have frequently asked three simple questions. The first is that all those present who have heard of Communism and who know that it exists should raise their hands. All hands are immediately raised. The second request is that all those present who are opposed to Communism and not ashamed to say so should raise their hands. Again all the hands shoot into the air. The vast majority of people readily affirm their opposition to Communism.

The third question I preface by the following remarks: "Be careful how you answer this question, for if you answer it in the affirmative, I will test you out by asking one further question. It will not be a difficult question, but if you cannot answer it, you have no right to answer this question in the affirmative. The third question is: Will those who know what Communism is please raise their hands?" One or two hands creep hesitantly and tentatively into the air. I then say, "Communism has a system of philosophic thought, an interpretation of being, a book of fundamental rules known as its philosophy. To the founders of Communism, this was the most important feature of their entire program. It underlies, unifies, integrates, and directs the apparently contradictory phenomena of Communist conduct and unites them into a purposeful whole. It is the major subject in every Communist school in the world. From it they derive their definitions of such terms as peace, truth, righteousness, justice, and democracy. If you do not understand something about the philosophy of Communism, you understand little about Communism itself. What is the name of the philosophy of Communism?"

This question elicits a considerable range of answers but seldom the right one. The answer is, of course, Dialectical Materialism. The Communists have made no secret of this. They have written it down, they have announced it to all the world, they teach it in every school that they control. Yet it is a somber fact that many anti-Communists have never even heard the name. Until recently, it was most unusual to find individuals in most groups who could so much as name their philosophy. Even today, the number of those who have any understanding of Dialectical Materialism is very small indeed.

One Sunday afternoon, by a peculiar accumulation of circumstances, I found myself speaking from the Communist platform in the Domain in Sydney, Australia. The Sydney Domain, a lovely park adjacent to the Sydney harbor, is possibly the world's greatest open forum. To this park each Sunday afternoon come all those with a message, real or imaginary, and there they harangue the passing throng. People gather in the thousands. The Communists always have a large, well organized meeting. As I spoke from the Communist platform, I mentioned Dialectical Materialism, whereupon the Communist leader challenged me. "What is Dialectical Materialism?" he asked. I replied, "Dialectical Materialism is the philosophy of Karl Marx that he formulated by taking the dialectic of Hegel, marrying it to the materialism of Feuerbach, abstracting from it the concept of progress in terms of the conflict of contradictory, interacting forces called the Thesis and the Antithesis culminating at a critical nodal point where one overthrows the other, giving rise to the Synthesis, applying it to the history of social development, and deriving therefrom an essentially revolutionary concept of social change." The questioner looked at me with wide-open eyes. I added, "Don't blame me. It is your philosophy, not mine. You are the one who believes it."

If we examine the philosophy of Dialectical Materialism in more detail, we see that there are two elements in it. There is the dialectical portion, and there is the materialist portion. Let us first consider briefly the materialism. The Communists are materialists. They affirm confidently, arrogantly, and repeatedly that there is nothing in the world except matter in motion. The precise form of their materialism was taken from the German philosopher, Feuerbach, a renegade theologian who forsook Theism and embraced materialism. His basic slogan was: "Man is what he eats. We are matter in motion, nothing more."

The argument between the materialist and the idealist is as

old as the history of human thought. Into the two categories, realists and idealists, the philosophers of the world have been divided. The realists or materialists contend that matter is the ultimate reality, and that thought is a secondary manifestation of matter. On the other hand, the idealists contend that matter is known only through thought. Take away thought and matter would be non-existent. The basic reality, therefore, is thought.

The following simple question is quite an effective instrument for distinguishing realists from idealists. The question is: Do the wild waves beating on the shore make a noise when no one is there to hear them? Those who believe that the wild waves do make a noise whether anyone is there or not are realists; those who believe that the wild waves make no noise unless someone is there to hear them are idealists. The realists believe that the noise is in the movement of the water itself; the idealists believe that it is a concept in some mind following the sensory mechanisms of perception. To the idealist, the noise is actually a manifestation of the mind. It is interesting to note that when this question is put to audiences, the realists or materialists usually outnumber the idealists by three to one.

It is to be noted that the word "idealism" bears no moral connotation. Since this word is associated in many minds with moral issues, it is difficult for those minds to divest the term of its moral attributes. In this sense the terms "idealist" and "materialist" refer merely to concepts of ultimate reality.

The Communists have no doubt as to where they stand. They are materialists. As far as Karl Marx was concerned, the idealist philosophers were simply the instruments of clerical reaction, servants of the clergy in their basic purpose of oppressing the working class in the interests of the Capitalist reactionaries. That disciple of Marx, Mao Tse-tung, expresses it thus: "There is nothing in the world except matter in motion." [1]

Most of the materialistic philosophers of Marx's day were mechanists. They believed that materialism allowed no room for

---

[1] Mao Tse-tung, *On Contradiction* (Peking: Foreign Languages Press, 1956), p. 16.

individual, volitional action. Their view was that all nature was automatic, that all actions were compulsory because of the forces that operated on the individual. Each man's destiny was beyond his control. Materialist philosophy thus resulted in nihilism in action and conduct. This philosophy is very well expressed by James Thomson in his poem, "The City of Dreadful Night," where he portrays man as the helpless plaything of the forces of nature.

> *If one is born a certain day on earth,*
> *All times and forces tended to that birth,*
> *Not all the world could change or hinder it.*

In marrying materialism to the Hegelian dialectic, Marx performed a remarkable operation. He brought into materialism an element of devotion, sacrifice, initiative, and purpose. He enunciated a deterministic, materialistic philosophy and, at the same time, brought into being intense, passionate dedication to make the inevitable come to pass. This is a truly remarkable Marxist achievement. If a group of people are utterly convinced that the sun is going to rise at 5:30 a.m. it should be a very difficult task to persuade these same people to awaken an hour early and work like slaves to make the sun do what they know it is going to do. Marx's achievement was somewhat similar to this. He took materialistic philosophy which taught that the force of history had decreed that certain things must inevitably happen, and married this philosophy to an intense personal, sacrificial dedication to make these things come to pass. He did this by introducing a mystical element from the Hegelian dialectic.

The German philosopher, Hegel, was the great philosopher of the early nineteenth century. His were the works and ideas which were discussed by the young intellectuals in the universities of that day. Hegel was an idealist, believing in the primacy of thought rather than of matter. Within the framework of his idealistic philosophy, he developed the dialectic. Hegel's philosophic thought is very difficult to understand. Hegel himself is reported to have said, "Only one man has understood me, and even he has not!" Marx contended that he was the one man who understood Hegel, and claimed that Hegel did not understand himself. Marx took the dialectical portion of Hegelian philosophy, married it to the materialism of Feuerbach, and produced dialectical materialism. Closely associated with him in his work was Frederick Engels who became his lifelong collaborator, co-worker, supporter, and interpreter. Together Marx and Engels built the philosophic basis of Communist practice.

FEATURES OF THE DIALECTIC

1. Progress

The first feature of the dialectic is the axiom that progress is inherent in change. The dialectic is a dynamic philosophy. It says that nothing is, that everything is in a state of flux or development. The dialectic would teach, for example, that no man can stand twice on the bank of the same river, for the second time it is a totally different river. In a similar way, everything is in process of development and change. Around us is a vast panorama of changing circumstances and conditions. Within the vastness of this change, there is a principle of developing organization, there is movement from lower to higher. Hidden within the diversity and apparent purposelessness of change there is a principle of progress.

The Communists make no attempt to prove that progress is at the heart of change. It is one of their axioms. They accept it by faith. In this sense, it is a pseudo-religious belief.

The word "progressive" has become one of their basic words. The Communist bookstore in Los Angeles is called the "Progressive" Bookstore. The last major political assault the Communists made on the presidency of the United States was through the "Progressive" Party. The Communists in labor unions always refer to themselves either as the "Militants" or the "Progressives."

The Communists apply this principle of progress in change to their own status within society. Liu Shao-chi writes:

> . . . the question arises: Can Communist society be brought
> about? Our answer is "yes." About this the whole theory of
> Marxism-Leninism offers a scientific explanation that leaves no
> room for doubt. It further explains that as the ultimate result of
> the class struggle of mankind, such a society will inevitably be
> brought about.[2]

They are the wave of the future. Their victory is as certain as
the rising of the sun because the same material law that causes
the sun to rise in the morning has ordained that they shall conquer and rule the world. Of this they have no vestige of doubt.

Since they believe this completely, their convictions are undis-
turbed by any evidence to the contrary that may appear day by
day. They stand above the changing scene of daily ebb and flow
and see the currents and tides of history. The idea that their
faith can be shattered by anything they see at present is naive to
the point of imbalance. Just how widespread the ignorance of
this is was revealed by many of the reasons advanced in support of Khrushchev's visit to the United States in September,
1959. An argument frequently put forward was: Let us show
Khrushchev how the people in America live; let him see their
fine homes, their modern automobiles, their open churches.
When he sees all this he will be impressed and will realize the
error of his previous viewpoint. Such an argument as this dis-
plays gross ignorance of Khrushchev's dialectical faith. In the
first place, Khrushchev's espionage system is such that he was
able to discover the most intimate secrets of American atomic
science. To imagine that he needed to come to America to discover how the American people lived, in what kind of houses they
lived and how many cars they had is utterly infantile. He was
equally well aware of the power and preparedness of America's
military might. But even if this were not so, even if Khrushchev's
tour of America had revealed to him many unsuspected facts
about the American way of life, none of these could have changed
him fundamentally. For present conditions and circumstances
have little authority to him. Khrushchev is a Communist, not because of the present, but because of the future. His life is gov-

---

[2] Liu Shao-chi, *How to be a Good Communist*, p. 38.

erned by a vision of the future. The future belongs to the Communists. They will inevitably conquer the world. You do not judge a building by the temporary scaffolding on which its builders walk. You see the vision in the mind of the architect.

An analogy may be drawn from the production of steel. The manufacturer promises a beautiful, burnished steel. In order to obtain this end product, the metal must go through certain dirty, unattractive stages. At one stage it is treated in the searing, flaming heat of the furnace. Were you to go to the manufacturer at this particular stage and say, "You have not kept your word. This is not steel. It is merely flame and heat. I can't use this!" he would look at you in utter amazement.

When the Communists listen to our arguments based on present circumstances and conditions, they must certainly be amazed, for their whole program rests on the future. Khrushchev was well aware of America's present wealth and power. He is reported as having said, "Anyone who does not know that America is rich and strong is unbelievably stupid." This realization merely confirms his faith in the greater glory of the future Communist state.

It is this future in which he is interested and in which he firmly believes. In the last analysis, he believes in the inevitable triumph of Communism not because of the evidence, but because of his faith in the dialectic. As a true believer he has lived and labored during forty years of sacrifice, danger and brutality.

2. The Dialectical Nature of Progress

The second feature of the dialectic is the nature of progress. Dialectical progress takes place in a certain pattern. The Communist slogan is: "Nature acts dialectically." Wishing to advance dialectically in a room full of people, I do not walk through the aisle and straight toward my goal. Nor do I move slowly through the crowd shaking hands with friends and acquaintances, discussing points of interest, gradually nearing the objective. The dialectical pathway is different. It consists of a resolute forward advance followed by an abrupt turn and retreat. Having retreated a distance there is another turn and advance. Through a series of forward-backward steps the goal is approached. To advance thus is to advance dialectically.

The Communist goal is fixed and changeless, but their direction of advance reverses itself from time to time. They approach their goal by going directly away from it a considerable portion of the time. Lenin wrote the textbook, *One Step Forward, Two Steps Back*. Chinese Communist schoolchildren are taught to do the dialectical march taking three steps forward and two steps back. If we judge where the Communists are going by the direction in which they are moving, we will obviously be deceived.

The Communist method of advance may be likened to the hammering of a nail. It is a very foolish person who brings the hammer down with a crashing, resounding blow and then keeps pushing. When the first blow has spent itself, back must go the hammer in preparation for the next blow. A person seeing the reverse movement of the hammer as an isolated act in time and not understanding the process of which this was a part, might find it difficult to believe that this hammer was driving in the nail. When he sees the backward swing as portion of a complete process, he realizes that the withdrawal is as important as the downward thrust to the realization of the objective.

For those not trained in dialectical thinking, it is very difficult to understand that the Communists have a fixed and changeless goal, but that their method of approach reverses itself all the time. The tendency is to judge where they are going by the direction in which they are moving. Many colleges taught, for example, that Communism as practised in Russia by Lenin and Stalin was a departure from Marx. They claimed that Marx's teaching had many good features about it, but that Lenin and Stalin put into practice something entirely different. Superficially the argument is reasonable. Take, for example,

Marx's teaching concerning marriage and what is practised in Russia with regard to marriage. Marx taught the abolition of marriage. The *Communist Manifesto* says:

> On what foundation is the present family, the bourgeois family, based? On capital, on private gain. In its completely developed form this family exists only among the bourgeoisie. But this state of things finds its complement in the practical absence of the family among the proletarians, and in public prostitution.
>
> The bourgeois family will vanish as a matter of course when its complement vanishes, and both will vanish with the vanishing of capital.[3]

In the light of this teaching, it might be expected that in Russia they would be weakening the family prior to its abolition. The truth is that they are presently strengthening the family. Divorce is discouraged; puritanic morals are encouraged; rewards are offered to those who have large families. They are strengthening the family in every way. Logically it would seem that since they are strengthening the family in Russia, they must have forsaken Marxism. The Communists, however, think and act dialectically. They realize that it is dialectical to approach their goal by going directly away from it. Their ultimate goal is to abolish the family. But they cannot abolish the family until they have changed human nature; they cannot change human nature till they control completely the environment that generates human nature; they cannot totally control the environment until they have conquered the world and destroyed the present environment; and they cannot conquer the world unless they develop a more courageous, more patriotic, more nationalistic people than their enemy. They have found by experience that they cannot develop a strong, nationalistic, patriotic people without encouraging a firm family base. They must therefore strengthen the family to develop the patriotism and courage of the people to increase the power of the Communist State so that they may conquer the world, establish a Communist dictatorship, and regenerate mankind. They will then abolish the fam-

---

[3] Karl Marx and Frederick Engels, *Manifesto of the Communist Party* (Moscow: Foreign Languages Publishing House, 1957), pp. 79-80.

ily. By strengthening the family, they are dialectically abolishing it. There is no inconsistency here. They are applying dynamic Marxism.

The same thing applies in the realm of religion. The ultimate goal of Communism is the abolition of all religion. Lenin says, "Atheism is a natural and inseparable portion of Marxism, of the theory and practice of scientific socialism. Our propaganda necessarily includes propaganda for atheism." It would be logical, therefore, to expect the persecution of religion wherever Communism is in power. In many places this is happening, but not in all. In some states under Communist rule, religion is being patronized and encouraged.

Religion constitutes a force that moves to action a certain segment of the Community. Communism utilizes existing forces. Religion, therefore, must be utilized to advance the final goal of Communism which is world conquest and thus contribute to its own destruction.

There are various ways in which religion may be used. They may instruct various members of the Party to join various religious faiths; for while it is quite impossible for a Christian to be a Communist, there is no inconsistency whatever in a Communist's professing Christianity to aid the triumph of Communism. As Khrushchev said to the French Socialists: "Some of our comrades are atheists in the Party and believers at home." One Communist, then, may be instructed to join the Catholic Church. He is told to be baptized, to believe everything he has to believe, to be the very finest Catholic imaginable and to secure influence in Catholic organizations. He will then have opportunity to influence Catholic organizations in a program which may appear to be completely unrelated to Communism but which may be important to their dialectical advance. Similarly, Communists are told to join various Protestant churches. Again they are to be fervently Protestant, orthodox to the core, ardent in spirit, and industrious in the program of that church. At the appropriate time, they too will be able to influence various church members and organizations for the Communist cause. Since to the

Communists none of these religious systems has any ultimate validity, but all of them constitute social forces which exist at present, there is nothing inconsistent in an atheistic Communist's being an apparently fervent religionist in the interests of the final Communist objective.

An Australian Episcopal delegation to Communist China found well-filled churches, and heard good sermons from apparently well-paid and contented preachers. Many reported that Christianity was flourishing in China. This report given by anti-Communists who were unaware of the Communist dialectic greatly helped the Communist cause. The Communist program for the church is threefold: to enslave, to utilize, and finally to destroy. The members of the delegation observed the phase of utilization. The initial stage of enslavement was brought about by extreme persecution. Genuine church leaders who were devoted to Christ were arrested, brainwashed, tried, and destroyed. The church buildings became halls in which accusation meetings were held rather than houses for the worship of God. When the church was thoroughly cowed and leaderless, a dialectical reverse took place and the persecution suddenly ceased. The Communists united all the non-Catholic churches into one organization which they called the Three Self Movement. They appointed a pro-Communist leader to formulate the policy of this organization; they appointed a Communist Commissar of Religion; and they paid the salaries of the preachers. Communist pressure was exerted to force everyone registered as a Christian to attend church. The preachers were obliged to meet twice a week with the godless Commissar of Religion to get the political line that they must proclaim on the following Sunday. One of the goals of the Three Self Movement is the liberation of Formosa. A certain Sunday could be designated "Liberate Formosa Sunday." The preachers, meeting with the political commissar would be given stories of the dreadful American persecution of their Chinese brethren in Formosa. They hear the tear drenched pleas of the Formosan people for their Chinese Communist brethren to come and liberate them. They are instructed to pass on this information to their congregations, and to offer prayers for the liberation of Formosa. The preachers have no way of knowing that these stories are not true. They live in a closed environment. All media of information are controlled by the Communist Party. Provided they obey instructions and follow the right political line, they may preach what they like. Visitors to China, therefore, see filled churches and hear good sermons by preachers who are well-paid and who are certainly not going to tell them anything that might bring back the previous period of persecution. If they are uninformed and unaware of the subtleties of the Communist dialectic, they will report that Christianity is flourishing in China.

The dialectic gives the Communists complete moral maneuverability. They may wear any garments. They may accept any faith. They may work to advance the self-interest of any nationalist or economic grouping. Their strategic mobility is effective indeed. Christians are prevented from following many courses of action by certain absolute standards. A Christian may not, for example, accept the Moslem faith, rise in the Moslem ranks, and then use his position to subvert Moslem customs and introduce Christianity. The Communists, however, have no absolutes. Their dialectical relativity gives them a total strategic mobility. They may adopt the coloring, the shape, the ideology, the morality, or the religious faith of any group. They become all things to all men that by all means they may enslave all.

3. Conflict

The third feature of the dialectic is the role of conflict in the process of change. According to the dialectic, the driving force in any situation is the conflict of two opposing forces. There is the established force called the thesis and there is the conflicting force called the antithesis. The conflict between these two forces is the dynamic of progress.

In dialectical language, everything is interpenetrated by its opposite. Nothing exists in isolation. You cannot have up without down; you cannot have plus without minus; you cannot have beauty without ugliness; you cannot have life without death. To every action there is an equal but opposite reaction. Everything exists in a state of conflict with its opposite. This conflict is the dynamic of being.

Initially this conflict gives a period of slow, relatively stable progress, a period of gradual change. This slow change never continues indefinitely. As change continues, a critical point is reached. At this point, certain things happen. Slow, gradual change gives way to rapid, fundamental change. In dialectical terminology, the antithesis negates the thesis; there is a transformation of quantity into quality and the emergence of a totally new direction of progress known as the synthesis. The synthesis now becomes the new thesis. The new thesis generates a new antithesis, and the new conflict between thesis and antithesis becomes the dynamic of the next stage of progress. Again a critical nodal point is reached. The new antithesis negates the new thesis and there is another transformation of quantity into quality. This is termed the Negation of the Negation and results in the emergence of a direction of progress parallel to the original one, but different in quantity and quality.

The Communists believe that this dialectical conflict or contradiction is universal in being. Mao Tse-tung writes in the introduction to his textbook on dialectics entitled *On Contradiction*: "The law of contradiction in things, that is, the law of the unity of opposites, is the most basic law in materialist dialectics." [4] Lenin said, "In its proper meaning, dialectics is the study of the contradiction within the very essence of things." [5]

The dialectic is very valuable to the Communists. It can be used to express in pseudo-logical form a conclusion empirically reached. It is a very valuable tool for deceiving the intellectuals and clothing with a pseudo-logic the edicts of the top Communist authority.

It was from the dialectic that Marx derived the doctrine of

---

[4] Mao Tse-tung, *On Contradiction*, p. 1.

[5] Lenin, *History of the Communist Party of the Soviet Union* (B), *Short Course,* English Ed. (Moscow: 1950), p. 133.

the inevitability of revolution as the climax of the class war. Surveying Capitalist society he said that the dynamic of Capitalism was a perfect illustration of the dialectic. Within Capitalism there are two conflicting forces: the bourgeoisie, consisting of the Capitalists who own the means of production, and the proletariat consisting of the workers in industry who labor for wages. Between these two forces there is a state of absolute, truceless conflict. The owners of the means of production want profit, while those who work for them want higher wages. If wages go up, profits come down. If profits go up, wages go down. Thus there is a fundamental conflict between these two groups, which Marx called the Class War. According to the dialectic, this state of conflict between Capital and Labor gives a period of slow, gradual change, but, inevitably, a critical point is reached. At this point, the slow, gradual nature of change disappears. It becomes rapid and violent. Revolution breaks out. Capitalist society is negated. There is a transformation of quantity into quality and the emergence of a new synthesis called Socialism.

The Communists are proudly revolutionary in theory and practice. The term "reformist" is to them a synonym for one who is ignorant of, and treacherous to historic reality. A reformist is so ignorant that he believes that fundamental changes in society can come about by slow, gradual means. The Communists are convinced that this cannot be, for they believe that history and nature declare that change must be wrought by revolution. To the Communist, the revolution is the golden experience of the future towards which they look with longing. As the bride looks forward to the day of her adorning, as the expectant mother looks forward to the day of her deliverance, so, with flashing eye and bated breath, with leaping pulse and exultant heart, the true Communist looks forward to the coming, glorious day of the revolution.

Communist belief in the inevitability of revolution is derived from the dialectic. Unless we understand the dialectic, we will be deceived on every hand. Unless we understand the dialectic, we cannot intelligently counteract Communism. When we do understand it, we are in a position to anticipate their actions and to take defense against them.

The most serious accusation that can be made against a Communist theorist is that he does not understand dialectics. With this accusation Stalin helped to destroy Bukharin. In Russia in 1928-29 there developed what Stalin termed the "Right Deviation" led by Bukharin. Bukharin was the brilliant Communist intellectual. Before the revolution, he had been a theorist comparable with Lenin himself. After the revolution, he occupied many important posts culminating in the leadership of the Communist International known as the Comintern. He was the author of the *ABC of Communism* and most authorities agree that he was the principal framer of "The Stalinist Constitution." His prestige and popularity among Communists were tremendous. It was thought by most people that he would emerge supreme in the struggle for power in 1928-29. When the climax of the struggle was reached, however, it was Stalin who had the votes. Finally Bukharin received the reward Stalin gave to most of his old comrades—a bullet in the back of the head.

Stalin had to find some justification for the ideological destruction of Bukharin. In the peculiar fashion of Communist theoretical debate, some quotation had to be found in the works of Marx, Engels, or Lenin that could be used against Bukharin. Stalin found his justification in a statement by Lenin. Stalin writes:

> Reference is made to a letter in which Comrade Lenin speaks of Bukharin as a theoretician. Let us read the letter.
> "Of the younger members of the Central Committee," says Lenin, "I should like to say a few words about Bukharin and Pyatakov. In my opinion, they are the most outstanding people (of the youngest forces), and regarding them the following should be borne in mind: Bukharin is not only a very valuable and important theoretician in our Party, he is also legitimately regarded as the favourite of the whole Party; but it is very doubtful whether his theoretical views can be classed as fully Marxian, for there is something scholastic in him (he has never studied, and, I think he has never fully understood dialectics)." *

---

* Words underlined were written in italics by Stalin.

Thus, he is a theoretician without dialectics. A scholastic theoretician. A theoretician about whom it was said: "It is very doubtful whether his theoretical views can be classed as fully Marxian." This is how Lenin characterized Bukharin's theoretical complexion.

You can well understand, comrades, that such a theoretician has still much to learn. And, if Bukharin understood that he is not yet a full-fledged theoretician, that he still has much to learn, that he is a theoretician who has not yet assimilated dialectics—and dialectics is the soul of Marxism.[6]

Upon this statement of Lenin, Stalin based his condemnation of Bukharin. Since Bukharin did not understand dialectics, he was second rate and could safely be destroyed.

The proof that Bukharin was not dialectical was to be found, according to Stalin, in his attitude towards the State. Communist theory taught that in the establishment of Communism, certain steps were necessary. A revolutionary situation had to be created, a violent revolution had to take place, and the bourgeois state had to be destroyed. The Communists had then to establish the dictatorship of the proletariat and to eliminate the residue of the bourgeoisie. When they had eliminated all possible counter-revolutionary elements of the old regime, the dictatorship could become less rigid and more benign, and begin to wither away. With the change of human nature, the dictatorship would become unnecessary and Socialism would turn into Communism.

Bukharin wanted to know why events in Russia were not following this pattern. He contended that in the eleven years since the revolution, they had consolidated their power, that they had liquidated all remaining members of the bourgeoisie, and that it was time that the powers of the dictatorship became a little less centralized and showed some signs of beginning to wither.

Stalin seized upon these views of Bukharin's as proof that Lenin had been right, that Bukharin was a scholastic who did not understand dialectics. Bukharin thought that the State was not withering away because it was growing stronger whereas,

---

[6] Joseph Stalin, *Problems of Leninism* (Moscow: Foreign Languages Publishing House, 1953), pp. 342-3.

according to Stalin, the fact that the State was growing stronger was the dialectical proof that it was withering away. Contradiction is the core of dialectics and dialectics is the heart of Marxism. When a baby is born, it immediately begins to wither, but the process of withering demands growth to maximum strength. The growth in strength of the Communist dictatorship was dialectical proof that it was "withering away."

Communist theory contains some strange dialectical anomalies. It teaches that Capitalism must change into Socialism by a "revolutionary" or dialectical process. Socialism will then evolve into Communism by a slow, non-violent, non-dialectical development. I have asked numerous Communist theorists the following question: "If Capitalism MUST change into Socialism by a dialectical process, why MUST Socialism turn into Communism by a non-dialectical process?" I have always been referred to some comrade of higher theoretical stature. I am still seeking the Communist theorist who can provide the answer.

The difficult, devious, and dangerous dialectic became the tool with which Stalin justified the murder of millions. Unless we understand it, it is probable that it may be used historically to justify the demise of all free peoples.

XI

PROGRAM FOR SURVIVAL

IT IS APPARENT that on the record to date, anti-Communist programs have completely failed to halt Communism. The Communists are riding high. Their program is in top gear. They are going from strength to strength.

Many groups think that they are successfully fighting Communism, but the record does not support their opinion. When giving evidence before the House Un-American Activities Committee in 1956, I was asked if I could name any unified, world-wide organization which was successfully fighting Communism. I replied that I could not do so. That reply has drawn more criticism than any other statement I made in that testimony. A number of groups have written in to rectify my ignorance on that point, and to tell me about their own organization which is successfully combatting Communism. No matter what the group, the measure of their success is limited indeed. The Communist program for world conquest continues to make phenomenal gains.

The fact is that progress is a relative thing. Many anti-Communist groups are moving in the right direction, but their progress up to the present time has been rather insubstantial. The degree of their success is somewhat similar to that of the missionary priest who had been working on a cannibal island. When asked what sort of success he was having, he replied, "Well, we are certainly making progress! Now the natives will eat only fishermen on Fridays." He was, perhaps, making progress, but it must be admitted that he had a long way to go.

For any program to be effective, there are three essential elements, namely, motivation, knowledge, and organization. Without adequate motivation, knowledge, and organization, any program must fail.

MOTIVATION

If people are to perform unpleasant tasks sacrificially and on a continuing basis, they must have a reason for doing so. An effective program against Communism demands time, money, energy and sacrifice. The first question to be considered is what motivating forces are available. What are the things which move people to action?

It is regrettably true that most people are moved most effectively by immediate, selfish interest. In most cases, self-interest dominates all other considerations. If a patriot wishes to arrange for an anti-Communist speaker to address a civic club or some corresponding group, there are two approaches which he may use. He may approach the program chairman with arguments such as these: "This man has a message your club should hear, a message which is vital to their businesses, to their homes, to their families, and to their very lives. It is your duty to have him bring them this message." Such an approach is likely to meet with little success. On the other hand, he may approach the program chairman and say, "Here is a good, entertaining, stirring speaker. Wherever he has spoken before, he has had a wonderful reception. He will really give you a good program." An approach like this is nearly always successful because it appeals to the self-interest of the program chairman. He wants to have people come up and pat him on the back for securing a good speaker.

This is true not only of civic clubs, but of all groups.

Churches, for example, have their own program and they are mainly concerned with the success of that program. You may approach a pastor with the argument that here is a message which is absolutely vital to his people. You may point out to him that Communism has conquered one billion people, far more than the Christian church has reached after its entire history; that Communism is rapidly closing the mission fields of the world; that Communism is the enemy of God, and that these things should be told to the people. Such an approach is not usually successful. You may, on the other hand, point out to the pastor that here is a man whom people like to hear and that if he holds a meeting in this church, he will attract into the church many people who do not normally attend. This is a very powerful argument and one which is apt to be successful.

Motivating forces must be found which are so powerful that they can overwhelm the lethargy, the immediate self-interest, the greed, and the routine that dominate so many lives. Life is a daily competition between conflicting interests for most intelligent and effective individuals. They must select from a host of matters clamoring for their attention those which appear to be the most urgent, the most entertaining, or which offer the greatest prospect of reward. The struggle against Communism must successfully compete with other matters clamoring for attention.

It would seem that a sufficient motivation would be found in the fact that a billion people under Communist control are being prepared to encompass the conquest and destruction of the Free World. The truth is, however, that generally speaking, an immediate motive of appetite or personal advantage will triumph over the long range, distant motivation of danger. To most people, Communism is still a long way off. It is causing a lot of trouble in many parts of the world, but it does not present, as far as they can see, a real, immediate threat to themselves or to their families.

A primary necessity, then, is an honest acknowledgment of the gravity of the danger. There must be a willingness to face the truth, avoiding the temptation to gloss over the dangers, or to take refuge in vain imaginations and pious phraseologies. The Communist enemy must not be sold short. Nothing is to be gained by a denial of his material assets, his strategic mobility and his inflexible determination to conquer.

There is certainly the danger that a true understanding of the perilous situation may lead some to the abyss of despair. The temptation is to shrug the shoulders and to declare that the task is hopeless. An alternative attitude is to search for some vast organization that can meet the danger. Responsibility is laid at the door of the government, the State Department, the military forces, or the churches. It is a rare individual who asks, "What can I do to avert disaster?"

Two students came up to me after I had spoken at a college in the Middle West. One of them was burning with anger. "How is it possible that our elected officials can be so ignorant?" he wanted to know. "It's their necks that are at stake! Why don't they do something?" I endeavored to redirect his attention from what the government should be doing to what he should be doing, but in vain. He was too filled with concern and anger against the government for its failure.

The second student reacted very differently. Said he, "Let's forget about the government and look at ourselves! I feel ashamed to think of the little I have done. I don't know just what I can do, but I am going to try to find out. I want to read and study and discover what I can do before I start worrying too much about somebody else." This is the kind of attitude that is needed. Each person must face his personal responsibility before he starts to criticize others.

When faced with this challenge, the average person raises the objection that the power of the individual is very limited. From one point of view, that is true; but from another point of view, what can be accomplished by individuals is unbelievable. Most of my time is spent trying to inform people and to arouse them to the Communist threat. However, even if I were to speak to a thousand people every night and could convince the thousand, it would take me five hundred years to speak to everybody now living in the United States, and I would go behind at the rate of two and a half million a year due to the continuing population increase. If, on the other hand, I were to speak to one person a week and could convince, inform and instruct that person, and if we each convinced, informed and instructed another person the following week, and the four of us each enlisted another the following week, by this process everyone in the world could be reached in less than twelve months.

The power of individuals is limitless. The time has come for people to cease looking for great organizations afar off, and to begin looking for things that can be done close at home. Every man who invites a friend into his home, gives him literature to read and informs him of the danger, is helping to thwart the Communist program. The powers of multiplication are limitless. The principle on which to work is the recruitment of individuals one by one on a basis of knowledge, understanding, and motivated service.

A stirring address at a mass meeting may stimulate the emotions and provoke great enthusiasm. Such a response is like a tropical thunderstorm that creates a flash flood rather than the consistent soaking the thirsty soil needs. The problem is to convert temporary emotional enthusiasm into sacrificial study and dedicated work. This is a difficult task and one that cannot be done on a mass basis.

A short time ago, I spoke to the legislature of one of the New England states. It was a magnificent meeting. My coming had been well prepared. The governor escorted me into the chamber. The chamber was packed and the galleries were filled. As I spoke, the legislators listened most attentively. When I had finished, they arose as one man in ecstatic, tumultuous, prolonged applause. The governor shook my hand. The legislators crowded round. One of them said, with the sparkle of a tear in his eye, "That was an emotional experience. I suffered with you." It was truly a great meeting.

That same evening, after a mass rally in a nearby city where I had spoken, the Attorney-General of that state came up to me and said, "I was dying to have you tell the people that this morning the legislature was shattered to its foundations, and that this afternoon, they went back to the real business of their existence: whether to have greyhound or horse racing in this state."

Many find it appalling that a situation of such gravity should be treated so casually. And yet this happens with ninety-nine out of every hundred who hear the message. This is the reality within which we must work. People will never be enlisted on a mass basis. They must be enlisted and trained one by one. If this is done, the powers of multiplication are miraculous.

The question of motivation is of basic importance in the struggle against Communism. It is not only a questioning of the forces that will motivate people in the United States, but a question of the forces that will move people in South America, Japan, Arabia, and India. What motives are adequate to make the people in these areas stand firm against the deceptive allurements of Communism? Despite its vital importance, this question of motivation has received very little attention.

I had occasion to address the Texas Legislature, and received the warm response so characteristic of the generous people of that state. After the address, one of the legislators came up to me and said, "India's the trouble! We must stop them from getting India!" He thought for a moment, and suddenly the answer came. It was the legislator's answer to all problems. Said he, "I've got it! We must spend a lot more money!"

"Let's think about that a moment," I replied. "You spent a lot of money in Iraq and Bolivia, didn't you? What did your money achieve in these countries? In Iraq, it provided the weapons with which the pro-Communists destroyed their enemies. In Bolivia, the American embassy personnel had to flee in shame from raging, Communist-led mobs. Your money does not seem to have done much good there, does it?"

All the money in the world is useless without dedicated personnel through whom it can be channelled. The great need is for dedicated, motivated personnel.

There are various motivations effective within a free society. A primary one is the profit motive. In its proper environment, this has been very effective. It has produced abundance, and has improved the material well-being of millions of people. There are certain spheres, however, in which it is quite inadequate as a motivating force. It certainly will not stir to selfless devotion the student intellectuals who are attracted to Communism. The appeal to them must be much more idealistic.

The problem of the Communist appeal to the student intellectual is one which money alone cannot solve. It is quite obvious that should a student rise in a university in Central or South America and say, "I'm opposed to Communism because it is against the interests of American big business," or even, "I'm against Communism because it will prevent my making a personal fortune," he would be scorned by a majority of his fellows. Reasons given for opposing Communism must be meaningful to the people concerned. People are needed who will oppose Communism in terms of an ideology that will command respect from the other students to whom they are speaking.

Such ideological forces are numerous. Forces that operate widely are religion, nationalism, morality, and love of family, as well as the desire to improve general economic well-being.

The great paradox is that people with a rich spiritual culture appear unaware of the motivating strength of spiritual forces and overwhelmingly convinced of the dominant power of the materialist motivation of improvement in economic conditions. On the other hand, the Communists boast of being complete materialists. They affirm there is nothing in the entire world but matter in motion. Nevertheless, they have shown a deep appreciation of the multiplicity of forces that lead groups of people to action, and have used these forces with great skill. The appeal of economic betterment has been by no means the only motive utilized by Communism. In actuality, they have made far more effective use of the appeal of nationalism.

The strange situation has developed in which the materialistic Communists are conquering the world with idealistic promises, while the professedly idealistic Free World is endeavoring to combat them with material gifts. An idea widely accepted by leading Americans is that Communism will not appeal to people with a degree of economic security. The policy adopted to combat Communism, therefore, is to improve the economic conditions of those who are still outside the Communist fold.

A program to combat Communism that rests upon such an economic foundation, is doomed. To feed the hungry and the poor is a Christian act. To assume that as a result of being fed, clothed, and housed they will automatically think the right thoughts and feel the right emotions is Marxism, not Christianity. A well-fed Communist is just as dangerous as a hungry one. He is likely to be more efficient.

There are things more important to many people even than life itself. The devout Hindu will feed his sacred cow while he starves to death. The devout Moslem will willingly die for Islam. There was a day when it was considered the normal thing for Christians to die for their faith. Powerful motivations indeed reside in religious faith.

Communism is the mortal enemy of these idealistic forces. It is the enemy of all religion. It will destroy the national integrity of every country. It will finally abolish home, family, and all moral codes. Here is a great unexplored pool of motivating forces for the struggle against Communism.

What must be realized is that government as practised in America has little access to these deep motivating forces. Constitutional government is limited government. There is strict separation of church and state. The government cannot directly mobilize a specific religious group in any land and utilize its motivating religious self-interest to thwart Communism. They would appear to be favoring one religious group as against another. Thus the role of the government in the struggle against Communism is limited. Individuals and groups of individuals can and must do what the government cannot do. The urgent need is to discover individuals and groups in all countries with motives that will lead them to effective service against Communism and to provide them with the knowledge and the tools of communication to make their work effective.

Students educated in the universities of the free countries have been among the most effective agents of Communism. The Communists have always realized the potential of such students, and have concentrated upon recruiting them, training them, and providing them with what they needed to serve Communism effectively in their own lands. For a number of years, it was almost routine for Australian Rhodes scholars who went to England to study, to return to Australia as dedicated Communists. Fortunately this tendency has eased off in recent years, but the Communist attempt to recruit the lonely foreign student continues, and is all too frequently crowned with success.

After I had spoken at a Mid-western university, I was somewhat startled when an exchange student from Afghanistan publicly and unashamedly extolled the virtues of Communism. His mentor was an American girl who sat by his side. He finished with the ringing assertion: "Communism is science. You said so yourself. The Communists say that any advance in science helps them. You must therefore acknowledge Communism or repudiate science."

I replied, "Arson is fire. I acknowledge it. Everyone knows it. I must therefore acknowledge arson and become an arsonist or repudiate fire to cook my meals and heat my home. Is that what you are trying to say?"

It is not enough to train students in technical science in American universities. They must be transformed into devotees of freedom. This can be done as they are the recipients, not only of knowledge, but of friendship and love. The student in a foreign land is often homesick and heartsore. The Communists provide not merely Marxist-Leninist ideology but also hospitality, companionship and social life. They make this lonely student feel they are interested in him as an individual, that he is important. When they have won him to Communism, they equip him with organizing skills and the necessary tools to serve Communism in his homeland.

We can and we must do likewise, not for Communist slavery, but for Christian liberty. This can be done. An illustration is found in the story of an exchange student from India whom I met in Seattle, Washington. He had just completed his degree as Doctor of Philosophy at the University of Washington. He was a handsome young Indian, a splendid student, and devoted to the principles of individual liberty. He was an evangelical Christian. Upon completing his degree, he was offered a job with the United Nations. He could have lived like an American gentleman, but he chose to return to his home in Kerala, India.

Shortly before his return, Kerala had become the first Indian state to elect a Communist government. It might have been expected that Kerala, the best educated and the most Christian of the Indian states, would have been the last state to elect a Communist government to power. The fact is, however, that the majority of the Christians voted Communist because of their ignorance of the true nature of Communism and the deceptive but glowing Communist promises.

He understood the nature and program of Communism. He determined to do what he could to inform his countrymen. Since the Communist government in Kerala was merely a state government which had to operate under the eye of the federal government and within the framework of the Indian constitution, the Christians still had their basic liberties. The Christian group to which he belonged began to publish a Christian magazine called *The Light of the World*. He and his helpers took the finest anti-Communist literature, translated it into the language of the people and circulated it in the very face of Communist terror. Their basic motivation was their informed Christian faith.

Some months later, I received a letter saying: "Do we really mean business? You and I know that the conquest of India is a step in the encirclement and surrender of America. The Communists are not conquering India with guns, bombs, and missiles, but with promises, photographs, magazines and newspapers. In Kerala we have a unique opportunity. The Communists will have to run for re-election. When this time comes, they can be expelled without violence if the people can be told the truth. The tragedy is that we have not the means to tell the people the truth. The Communists have many daily newspapers, and large numbers of magazines. Can you help us to get a daily newspaper dedicated to truth, democracy, and freedom and resting on a Christian foundation?" In reply to my question about costs, he said that it would take $50,000.

Raising such a sum of money posed something of a problem. I sought help from one of the very large foundations in New York. I had been told that the members of this foundation were interested in India. The officials were courteous and friendly. They listened with great interest to the program, and commended it highly. Then they said, "Magnificent as the project is, much as we commend it, we cannot help you because you are Christian. We cannot get mixed up in religion in India."

I tried to argue with them. "Can't you see what you are doing? You have told me yourselves that you have difficulty securing anyone to go to India representing your group unless you increase his salary by twenty-five per cent. When that individual with his increased salary gets to India, what does he do? Does he go out into the villages where the temperature may be 120 degrees in the summer, where the drinking water may be filled with dysentery, bacilli and amoebae? Or does he sit in an air-conditioned room at some hotel and write reports?

Each year the Communists appoint thousands of fulltime Communist agents, primarily recruited from students who are motivated, dedicated, and thoroughly indoctrinated with Communism. They equip them with beautiful literature, and send them round the villages to deceive the people by offering them heaven on earth. We do not have thousands, but we do have some hundreds who have a motive to sacrifice in the fight against Communism. Communism is the enemy of their God, their Christ, and their freedom. Because of this, they are willing to go to their people and warn them of the dangers of Communism. You may not approve of their motive, but surely you approve what they are doing. Yet you are saying, 'We cannot help them because they are Christian. We cannot help them because they have a motive. Take away their motive so that they won't do it, and then maybe we can help them to do what they won't do.'"

Despite this discouraging response, we determined to accept the challenge and help our Indian Christian friends in their struggle which is also our struggle. The first edition of this paper was published in August, 1959.

Shortly before the publication of this first edition, crisis hour arrived in Kerala. The Communist government of Kerala was expelled by the central government, and elections were scheduled to take place within six months. The newly born newspaper was thus faced with tremendous responsibility and opportunity. This came about because a group possessed of motivation and knowledge received the material aid needed to be effective. Within a free society, motivations are multiple and may even appear contradictory. They must be utilized and not destroyed.

My personal motivation is twofold. In the first place I have a wife and family whom I love very dearly. The Communists consider them diseased social animals. At present rates of progress, Communism will have conquered the world within a generation, and, as members of the residual diseased bourgeois class, my wife and family will become historically redundant with obvious ugly implications.

In the second place, I have a Christian faith. I believe in God and His love, Christ and His redemption, and the great commission to go into all the world and preach the gospel. Communism is the enemy of God and of Christ and His gospel. These two facts have motivated me to do everything within my power to stay the advance of Communism.

Others share this motivation. A brilliant orthopedic surgeon was faced with the facts about Communism. He said to me: "I wake up every morning and I see one billion people encircling us for our conquest and our destruction. I don't like it, so I assume that it cannot be so and try to put it out of my mind. I have been trained to examine evidence and face facts, and the evidence keeps returning to haunt me. I examine it and I cannot escape it. I then examine my own life. I look at my wife and children and I say, 'What am I doing to preserve their future?' Certainly I am building a good surgical practice, acquiring a good name, getting a good bank balance, but what will that matter if the Communists take over? The only thing that is important is stopping the Communists, and I am not doing anything to do that. I don't know what to do but I intend to find out and when I do find out, I don't care what it costs. By God's grace, I'll do it." He is ready to leave home, country, and economic security to do his duty to his home and country.

If the facts about the Communist advance are true, his attitude is not merely praiseworthy, it is perfectly reasonable and intelligent. The trouble is that most people simply do not believe these facts. They think they do, but actually they do not. If they were convinced, they would be prepared to pay any price and spend any amount of time and money to try and avert the threat. Until our actions match our professed beliefs, onlookers can be forgiven for denying our sincerity and despising our hypocrisy.

KNOWLEDGE

The finest motivation is impotent without adequate knowledge. For generations mothers have longed to be able to protect their children from the scourge of poliomyelitis, but they could not do it because they did not know how. Only out of knowledge acquired from continuing study has a program to combat it emerged. It is possible to hate Communism fervently and simultaneously to serve it faithfully and well. Those who spread poliomyelitis hated it, but that did not prevent their disseminating it. They did not even know they were spreading it. The same kind of thing is happening with Communism. It is being spread far and wide by people who do not know what they are doing.

When people are found who are motivated and concerned, they must be given knowledge. One way in which this may be done is through literature. The literature on the subject of Communism is extensive. It must be studied. Invaluable training can be gained in study circles where discussion aids in true understanding. There is no substitute for specific knowledge.

Communism should be taught in the schools but it should be taught with a moral directive. It should not be taught as an alternative economic philosophy but as a system of tyranny. The object of the teaching should be to protect the students against the deceptive subtleties of Communist dialectics and to promote within them a greater devotion to freedom. It should be taught as a medical school teaches cancer or tuberculosis—as an aid to its elimination.

Teaching that merely compares and contrasts certain features of Capitalist and Communist economics is dangerous indeed. In a free society, the students continuously enjoy the privileges of freedom and it is difficult for them to conceive of a system where these values do not prevail. Isolated aspects of Communist economics assume a glittering luster when illuminated by the radiance of the star of liberty. In the environment of Communist tyranny, they are tawdry and repulsive.

Khrushchev told the American people that in Russia they are on the verge of abolishing income tax. Within American society that seems a highly desirable goal. To abolish income tax under Communist tyranny is a sham and delusion. The big American corporations do not need to tax their employees. The Communist Party is the monopoly corporation that owns the entire Russian economy. It fixes all wages and prices. It can impose a one hundred per cent sales tax without announcing it in any way.

If students are taught that Communist economy can run without income tax and are not taught the tyrannical role of the Communist Party, great damage is done. At an early age, each student should be taught that the issue is clear cut—freedom versus slavery. They then should be taught the techniques by which Communism seeks to deceive, conquer, and enslave.

Love without knowledge is frequently impotent. I had been speaking to a church group in California about the necessity for knowledge. Following the message, the minister stood up to give a devotional, apparently in the hope that he could counteract any bad influence I might have had. The theme of his devotional was that love is the greatest force in the world. He said that we are told to love all God's children. Everybody is God's child. The Communists are God's children. We should therefore love the Communists. Khrushchev is God's child. We should love Khrushchev.

After the meeting we fell into conversation. He was apparently conscious that what he had said might have appeared as rebuttal of what I had stressed, that is, the need for knowledge. He said that this had not been his intention, but that I had seemed to exalt knowledge above love. I told him that as far as I was concerned, he had not said anything, for love cannot operate without knowledge. If a mother spends all her time kissing her child and fails to have it inoculated against polio, has she shown love towards it? Suppose you see an insane hoodlum kicking a little girl to death a hundred yards down the street. Before you can get there, the little girl will be dead. In your hand you have a gun. How do you show love in a situation like that?

What is needed is not pious phraseology, but a loving spirit and the knowledge to apply it in a given situation. Love without knowledge is blind, and knowledge without love may lack dynamic power. We need a synthesis of love and knowledge. Then truth shall prevail.

Any program to combat Communism must be based on a thorough study of the Communist mind, motives and techniques. When we understand these, we can see clearly in the murk of the Communist dialectic, detect the tactic of the enemy and devise a program to abort his plans.

ORGANIZATION

Organization is the genius of Communism. Communism is the triumph of organization over undirected economic and social forces. It is a truism that organization will prevail over disorganization. An anti-Communism program needs organization.

A commonly held view is that unity is the great need in this organized anti-Communism program. An argument such as the following is assured of a tumultuous reception with almost any group of businessmen: "Communism is the universal enemy. It is the enemy of every segment of a free society. It is the enemy of both Management and Labor. It is the enemy of all religions; Protestant, Catholic, Jewish, Hindu and Moslem. Since it is the enemy of all free political parties, it is the common enemy of Republican and Democrat. Since it is our universal enemy, it should cause us to submerge our differences and unitedly throw ourselves into the struggle against it." Such an argument will be cheered to the echo yet it is as phony as a three dollar bill. When groups submerge their differences, they frequently submerge their motivating forces and the organization so formed is like an automobile without gasoline because the dynamics of action reside in the submerged differences.

Suppose, for example, a joint Catholic-Protestant organization is formed. The liberty of the Catholic conscience necessitates freedom to propagate the doctrines of the faith. The liberty of conscience of an evangelical Protestant depends upon his freedom to preach the gospel of Christ. If the Protestant gets into an organization where he must refrain from preaching the gospel, and the Catholic in that organization must refrain from advancing Catholicism, both are embarrassed, and rendered so much less effective. If, however, they are in different organizations where the consciences of both are clear, they can do far more effective work.

The Christian Anti-Communism Crusade held a school for anti-Communists in the educational building of the Tower Grove Baptist church in St. Louis, Missouri. The school was attended by a considerable number of Catholics. After the school, the Catholics were very eager to form a joint Protestant-Catholic anti-Communist organization. I replied that, should we do so, each would paralyze the effectiveness of the other. Each group has a dominant purpose. The emotional attitudes of the members are tuned to the fulfillment of that purpose. Unless the message is in tune with that purpose, it will not produce the maximum result. Opposition to it may be unconscious, but it will be real nevertheless. If the message against Communism is tuned to the basic purposes of the organization, it will rally the enthusiastic support of the group. When an organization consists of elements with contradictory purposes, it is difficult to mobilize the enthusiastic support of all elements. Maybe this should not be so, in relation to such a universal enemy, but as a practical issue, it is so.

I suggested that the Catholics form a Catholic organization so that they could speak to Catholics without the embarrassment of a Protestant leader. Rather hesitantly, they agreed, and formed the Cardinal Mindszenty Foundation. This organization is now doing a most effective work and its leadership is now convinced of the wisdom of the course pursued. Instead of uniting, Catholic speaks to Catholic, and Protestant speaks to Protestant. Information is shared. Joint projects may be undertaken. But organizational unity is not sought. Neither infringes his conscience. Each has the dynamic of his faith, and can be much more effective than if a united organization had been formed.

Organizational unity is a mirage. The great need is multiplicity, not unity. The unity of a free society resides in its diversity. Movements must be formed which conserve the motivating forces within each group and channel them into the struggle for freedom and survival. The Communists understand this very well. That is why they operate through a great number of front organizations, each of which is tuned to some specific motivating dynamic. Every religious, professional, economic, and cultural group should organize an anti-Communist program.

There is always the temptation to try to form a totalitarian organization modelled on Communism. After I had spoken at a school in Eugene, Oregon, I received a letter from one of the students which began, "Dr. Schwarz, you hypocrite! You came to us and you showed us the power of Communist organization, their dedication, their devotion, and their discipline. You told us how the Communist leader can sit and order every individual to do a certain task, and how the individual obeys whatever the cost. Then you start an organization with a membership fee of $10 a year, and life membership at $100. How will you ever combat them like that? Let's form an organization like that of the Communists where we have discipline and authority and where people do what is necessary at whatever cost to themselves."

I replied that I appreciated the spirit of his letter. I did not object to his calling me a hypocrite, for I often felt that way myself. Yet I was afraid that he did not fully understand the conflict between totalitarian organization and the Christian liberty of conscience. This liberty of conscience itself should direct the individual into unselfish service to fulfil his responsibility towards God and to the preservation of that liberty for all men. Any organization that flouts this principle is anti-libertarian and anti-Christian. Discipline must be largely self-discipline; sacrifice must be voluntary, not compulsory. The mainspring of our organization must be from within the character of free citizens.

I cannot compel you to do anything in this struggle. God Himself renounced His right to compel. It depends upon voluntary choice and freewill.

Who will win? The Communists are supremely confident of complete victory. They claim that their victory is assured because of the quality of character in democratic lands. They affirm that the environment generating this character is Capitalism in its dying phase. Since Capitalism is dying, it creates character without survival virtue. They are convinced that the average citizen of the Free World is so intellectually lazy and dishonest, so greedy and selfish, so intoxicated with entertainment, so consumed with his immediate problems that no matter how clear the evidence of impending doom, that evidence will never be acknowledged, and the organizational steps necessary for survival will never be taken.

We categorically reject this claim. We are not the helpless victims of our environment, doomed to destruction. The fault lies not in our environment but in ourselves. The political, judicial, educational and cultural organizations of ə free society can function only when the individual citizens have enlightened minds and are dedicated to the foundations of freedom. The basic responsibility rests on each one. The success of this book can be measured by the number of readers whose attention has been redirected from the responsibility of others to their own responsibility; who are asking the question, "What can I do?" Upon such a foundation the political, legislative and cultural programs necessary can be built.

Material forces alone do not determine the destinies of men. The resources of an infinite God can change the balance of material assets. These resources are liberated through the prayer, the sacrifice, and the intelligent organization of people filled with the love of God. Fundamentally, the problem is a moral and spiritual one. The foundations of freedom must be girded with a moral and spiritual revival. As free men humbly seek God and present their bodies, minds and hearts to their country and the cause of all mankind, we may well believe that tyranny shall not triumph and freedom shall not perish from the earth.

INDEX

21135